On Arrogance

This book explores the notion of arrogance from a broadly psychoanalytic perspective, and examines its importance in the consulting room and the wider world.

Starting from the writings of Freud and Bion, Civitarese explores how much our inner and outer worlds may be shaped by arrogance, both our own and that of others. The author proposes that much of psychological suffering can be explained by non-recognition, of our own needs and desires, or those of others. It can be argued that arrogance is a symptom of lack of mutual recognition and in itself a significant obstacle to psychic growth. This book is an interdisciplinary dialog between psychoanalysis, literature, and philosophy, which offers a non-reductive view of arrogance to make visible the psychological suffering it conceals.

With a broad psychoanalytic basis, *On Arrogance* will be essential reading for psychoanalysts, psychotherapists, scholars in humanities, and anyone wishing to broaden their understanding of arrogance in clinical work and beyond.

Giuseppe Civitarese, MD, PhD, is a psychiatrist, training and supervising analyst of the Italian Psychoanalytic Society (SPI), and member of the American Psychoanalytic Association (APsaA) and International Psychoanalytic Association (IPA). He lives, and is in private practice, in Pavia, Italy.

Psychoanalytic Field Theory Book Series
Giuseppe Civitarese
Series Editor

The *Psychoanalytic Field Theory Book Series* was initiated in 2015 as a new subseries of the *Psychoanalytic Inquiry Book Series*. The series publishes books on subjects relevant to the continuing development of psychoanalytic field theory. The emphasis of this series is on contemporary work that includes a vision of the future for psychoanalytic field theory.

Since the middle of the 20th century, forms of psychoanalytic field theory emerged in different geographic parts of the world with different objectives, heuristic principles, and clinical techniques. Taken together they form a family of psychoanalytic perspectives that employ the concept of a bi-personal psychoanalytic field. The *Psychoanalytic Field Theory Book Series* seeks to represent this pluralism in its publications. Books on field theory in all its diverse forms are of interest in this series. Both theoretical works and discussions of clinical techniques will be published in this series.

The series editors are especially interested in selecting manuscripts that actively promote the understanding and further expansion of psychoanalytic field theory. Part of the mission of the series is to foster communication amongst psychoanalysts working in different models, different languages, and different parts of the world. A full list of titles in this series is available at: https://www.routledge.com/Psychoanalytic-Field-Theory-Book-Series/book-series/FIELDTHEORY

On Arrogance

A Psychoanalytic Essay

Giuseppe Civitarese

 Routledge
Taylor & Francis Group

LONDON AND NEW YORK

Designed cover image: © 'Oedipus and the Sphinx, Gustave Moreau (1864). Bequest of William H. Herriman, 1920. Public domain, courtesy of The Met Fifth Avenue https://www.metmuseum.org/'.

First published 2024
by Routledge
4 Park Square, Milton Park, Abingdon, Oxon OX14 4RN

and by Routledge
605 Third Avenue, New York, NY 10158

Routledge is an imprint of the Taylor & Francis Group, an informa business

British Library Cataloguing-in-Publication Data
A catalogue record for this book is available from the British Library

ISBN: 978-1-032-66939-7 (hbk)
ISBN: 978-1-032-67711-8 (pbk)
ISBN: 978-1-032-66942-7 (ebk)

DOI: 10.4324/9781032669427

Typeset in Times New Roman
by KnowledgeWorks Global Ltd.

Contents

Introduction

Why write about arrogance? If we look at the public square of television and other media, Twitter, Instagram, Facebook, etc., we get the impression that we are not just talking about a character trait of some people, but about something that has become almost a collective value, that is, a model of acceptable behavior, even desirable and to be imitated. The spectacle is embarrassing. No one is ashamed of being or looking arrogant anymore. Friendliness, respect, listening, moderation, and hospitality have become obsolete.

This is not just an Italian phenomenon. In politics, it is particularly characteristic of those with nationalist tendencies, which have recently become widespread in all parts of the world, even where we would least expect them. Who would have thought that in countries where people are extremely careful not to use terms that offend ethnic minorities, someone could come to power who seems to have no such problems? Of the two extremes represented respectively in the novels *The Human Stain*, in which Philip Roth[1] stigmatizes the intolerance inherent in the excesses of political correctness, and *The Plot Against America*, in which he imagines an authoritarian drift of the nation, it is certainly the second that worries us most. And again, in other civilized countries would we ever have imagined, in the name of restoring national sovereignty, a certain deliberate, systematic, and harsh policy perpetrated against new immigrants and so-called "immigrants" who have actually been there for years?

The explanation that comes to mind is that arrogance is an element of a statistically tested and cynically applied communication strategy designed to take center stage by appealing to people's most regressive instincts. Why? Because it "works". What counts is to unsettle the interlocutor and, if necessary, not to refrain from raising one's voice and insulting him. At the

DOI: 10.4324/9781032669427-1

same time, it serves the purpose of rejoicing in such behavior and despising anything that smacks of education, competence, gentleness, humility, and respect. The arrogant person does not know where doubt or courtesy belong.

But arrogance is not just about political, economic, media, and cultural power. In a broader sense, in our country, at the level of society, arrogance is an ethereal, intangible "mafia" mentality. It has the extraordinary ability to take on a thousand forms. The list would be long: from the amoral familism of which Moravia spoke, to the little everyday incivilities, from the systematic disregard for merit in institutions that should instead take great care of it, since it is the basis of their very existence, to the little abuses of bureaucracy, and so on.

It is often the case that not even the intellectuals, or at least those who call themselves such, behave any differently. In theory, they are supposed to be the critical conscience of society. In practice, they are often enslaved by the corporate and mercantile logic of the culture industry. Even philosophy struggles to free itself from the marketing system. Sometimes it even degenerates into improvised operations, fashions, and trends, in which it would be difficult to recognize any real substance of thought.

Although motivated by some annoyance with the aspects of incivility that I have listed, the trigger that led me to think about arrogance is entirely incidental. In fact, it arose as a natural extension of my interest in a 1958 text by Wilfred R. Bion entitled "On Arrogance". It is an essay of only six pages, but it marks a turning point in the history of psychoanalysis and gives us a new key to interrogate the concept of arrogance on several levels simultaneously. This is why I deal with arrogance not as a moralist but as a psychoanalyst. This does not mean that I do not try, when necessary, to enter into dialogue with other disciplines in order to achieve, if possible, a more integrated view of things.

In terms of essays,[2] there is almost nothing to read on the subject. It is true, however, that if we identify it with the ancient concept of *hýbris*, it has always been at the heart of Western culture, as a kind of original sin. Hence the idea that it can function as the theoretical site where points of view belonging to different fields and disciplines such as psychology, philosophy, literature, sociology, and political theory, can meet productively and contribute to the always necessary and urgent diagnosis of the "bad present".[3]

In fact, I am a great believer in interdisciplinary exchange. No one can claim to be a master of more than one discipline. When you venture beyond the boundaries of specialization, you always run the risk of a certain super-ficiality. But it is also true that each person brings a particular experience and sensitivity to the dialogue. In the most fortunate cases, this makes it possible to notice aspects and resonances that the super-expert locked in his academic fortress would not notice. In particular, there is an extraordinar-ily fruitful tradition of exchange between psychoanalysis and philosophy.[4]

In reality, the issues they address are often the same, albeit from differ-ent perspectives and with different methods. In this book, I therefore find myself constantly weaving cross-references between issues that are close to my heart because they are relevant to my daily work as a clinician, such as the relational nature of the therapeutic process, and ideas of some contem-porary authors that I appreciate, such as Derrida, Foucault, Butler, Pinkard, Brandom, Mancini, and classics such as Hegel. Hegel in particular, and in the last century Husserl and then Merleau-Ponty, are of enormous inter-est to psychoanalysis because of how they develop the theme of intersub-jectivity. Couldn't this attempt to transcend the caesuras between different knowledge be a way of staging, in this case in theoretical work, a first form of the "recognition" of the other that is at issue throughout the book?

For example, in the first chapter I explore some definitions of arrogance, also using literary figures. As an authentic form of knowledge of human life forms and their complexity, literature allows us to move from the two-dimensional, abstract level of conceptual definition to the three-dimensional level of an affective or 'aesthetic' vision. Not without some surprise, I real-ized that there are not many truly exemplary "arrogant" characters. Some, however, are absolutely "outstanding". For example, Sophocles' Oedipus is a character who introduces the next chapter.

In the second chapter I examine Bion's text in detail. My thesis is that we can think of it as an original commentary on Sophocles' *Oedipus Rex*; as the announcement of the discovery of certain larval forms of psychosis; as a reflection on the essence of psychosis in general; finally, as the diagnosis of a possible 'disease' of psychoanalysis itself. Oedipus, the analyst who identifies with his figure, and the psychotic would suffer from the same triad of symptoms, Bion argues: arrogance curiosity stupidity. In common, they would all have the impulse to want to know the truth "at any cost".

In the essay, Bion redefines the Oedipal crime no longer in terms of sexu-ality, but in terms of the epistemic instinct—Foucault would call it the "will to know"—that leads him to solve the riddle of the Sphinx. By analogy, the "psychosis" of the analyst (or of psychoanalysis) would be expressed in the desire to be "scientific" (as opposed to hermeneutic) and to tell the patient what he unilaterally believes to be the truth. Anticipating similar themes in *Transformations* and *A Memoir of the Future*, in *On Arrogance* Bion lays the groundwork for a critique of possible ideological aspects of psychoanalysis, and at the same time offers possible correctives.

My attempt to understand the nature of arrogance does not come from an abstract discourse, but, following Bion, from the specific ground of the theory and practice of analytic treatment, on the one hand, and from the experience of the institutional life of psychoanalytic societies, on the other. The main idea is to learn from experience and to propose, as a key to interpreting the present, the model of how it is possible to achieve an 'ethical re-foundation' of psychoanalysis (as a theory, clinical practice, and institution) that will allow it to guard against its own 'arrogance' and to better fulfill its vocation. Indeed, if it is plausible that psychoanalysis is one of the articulations of the power-knowledge of sexuality, as highlighted by Foucault, it is also true that, in relation to this power, it is at the same time one of the most incisive points of resistance.

Within psychoanalysis, my particular perspective is that of the post-Bionian theory of the analytic field.[5] In my view, it is a contemporary and effective tool for the treatment and self-healing of psychoanalysis. Indeed, it succeeds in providing a broad and convincing view of the dynamic balance between subjectivity and intersubjectivity that underlies the well-being of the person and society. Above all, this theory is inspired by its own radical principle of indeterminacy. In the analytic interaction, this principle gives way to a focus on the participation not only of the patient but also of the observer-analyst. This theoretical perspective, along with others, contributes to the radical renewal that psychoanalysis needs. What is needed is a new paradigm based not only on the goodwill or good feelings—certainly, we would say with Derrida,[6] not the "arrogance of so many 'clean consciences'"—but a more agile and versatile critical and self-critical sensitivity.

In the third chapter, I attempt to "update" Freud's *Civilization and Its Discontents*[7] in an attempt to interpret what we might call the new malaise of civilization. In order to diagnose and take a position on the arrogance that manifests itself in protean ways in society, I take as a model Bion's denunciation of the 'arrogance' of psychoanalysis and the 'cure' it proposes. In contrast to speculative thinking, psychoanalysis faces the problem of how to translate its insights into a practice of healing. If I have a certain idea of splitting as the source of suffering, I have to work out appropriate technical devices to resolve it.

If, for example, I believe that the split can be recomposed from a relationship based on authentic forms of mutual recognition—as can only happen on an equal basis, outside relationships of domination, hierarchy, and judgment—then I have to draw the consequences. If I believe that our way of conceiving the therapeutic relationship is still unbalanced in the sense of a relationship of inequality, then I have to build the appropriate theoretical and technical tools to make this moment of symmetrization of the relationship actually become a dimension of care and a concrete existential possibility. Using this analogical, indirect way of dealing with the theme of the malaise of civilization, and without renouncing the interpretive boldness that only a discipline with a speculative soul allows, nevertheless allows me—I repeat—to remain on the ground that I know from experience, which is that of clinical practice.

Finally, before the brief note entitled "Conclusions", in which I summarize the entire course of the book, in the fourth chapter I try to look at the concept of "recognition" with an even higher resolution, if possible; or rather, using the binocular vision that speculative and psychoanalytical perspectives offer me, at recognition-*at-one-ment*. In fact, the concept of *at-one-ment* corresponds roughly to what Hegel means by recognition (*Anerkennung*). Not surprisingly, Hegel inspired Lacan's intersubjectivism and his conception of the unconscious and its relation to language, as well as much of relational psychoanalysis.

Not only arrogance but every form of psychological suffering, whether of the individual or of society, in my view arises from traumatic experiences of non-recognition. For Hegel, however, the failure of recognition is primarily arrogance. To dwell on arrogance from this point of view, also because of its "normality", and indeed because of the success it seems to have as a communicative code in our society, allows us to see this issue in a new light. In a nutshell, the main thesis of the book is that arrogance is the antithesis of recognition and the most banal form in which evil can manifest itself.

In principle, we should be wary of extending psychoanalysis into areas of research other than its specific field, which is the treatment of mental suffering. However, we must give Freud credit for giving it the character of a critical theory of society.[8] *The Future of an Illusion, Group Psychology and the Analysis of the Ego, Civilization and its Discontents*, etc., anticipate the current of philosophy called Critical Theory that Adorno and Horkheimer would inaugurate with the Frankfurt School and from which they would take their name. Even today, Freud's political writings illuminate the present with the dazzling light of the brilliant insights scattered throughout their pages. Even when we disagree with him, his vision does not allow itself to be archived. Instead, it continues to question us, to make us doubt the arrogance inherent in all that is presented as obvious and self-evident.

This is the dimension to which Barthes[9] refers with the concept of *doxa*. In this, Freud shows an extraordinary relevance. Is there anything in philosophy, and in non-fiction in general, even remotely comparable to Freud's powerful exploration of the possibilities of realizing human happiness? Are we really sure that we can safely dismiss Freud's "mythological" concept of the death drive? And if not, how might it be reinterpreted from a contemporary perspective?

Secondly, what legitimizes the extension of psychoanalytic knowledge to the larger society is the fact that individual and social neurosis (and psychosis) have the same structure. As Freud[10] writes, all psychology is social psychology. Indeed, as group-specific, there is no need to admit a "social drive", since it would be perfectly isomorphic with the same "social drive" that governs the "group" of voices heard in the conscious and unconscious theatre of the individual's mind. For Bion, this drive can be understood as the system of "valences"[11] which, first at the level of instinctual and pre-reflexive intersubjectivity, and then also at the level of reflexive or purely linguistic intersubjectivity, drives individuals to establish links between themselves, thus allowing the other to access the self and vice versa.

A synonym for this "force" could be the "truth drive", the only concept of drive that Grotstein[12] identifies in Bion's thought: the need of human beings, just as they draw oxygen from their breath and nutrients from their digestion, to supply the mind with micro- and macro-experiences of unity or emotional attunement: elementary units of sense and meaning that are essential to exist as beings endowed with self-consciousness and to have a world. Freud[13] does not accept the "hypostasis" of a collective psyche, even if one cannot help attributing an organization to it. He does not believe that such a collective psyche could ever be independent of the psychic processes taking place in the individual. But today—revealing a limitation of his theory of the unconscious—we would say that the reverse is also true. It would be equally inadmissible to hypostatize the psyche of the individual (as isolated in itself), although one could not fail to recognize in it an organization. In fact, to paraphrase Freud, we could not even attribute to it an independence from the psychic processes that take place in the group or in the dimension of sociality. The individual unconscious is in itself "collective" and infinite,[14] and thus transcends the individual. From this point of view, it becomes impossible to oppose the unconscious of the group to the unconscious that is supposedly "closed" and hermetically encapsulated in a given subject.

In order to carry out my investigation of arrogance, I adopt the practical method of giving several definitions of it and in relation to different contexts: as an extemporaneous behavior, as a character trait, as a symptom (all referring to both the individual and society); and finally, as a 'structural' element of what we call civilization. This approach involves some repetition and may give the impression of discontinuity. However, it has the advantage of allowing individual chapters or sections to be read independently. My intention is that each new definition 'negates' the previous one, but also affirms it and raises it to a level of greater complexity. So at each step, arrogance takes on a new meaning, but one that resonates with the previous ones and casts them in a new light. In all the different meanings, we will see that at the heart of arrogance, there is always the same movement of abstraction, of splitting,[15] of separation, of emptying the concrete, of detachment from living thought, of isolation from affect, of neo-proliferation of the intellect at the expense of corporeality, of fixation or crystallization of thought, of obstinate and mechanical rationality. Abstract logic is not dialectical, it sees contradiction but does not respect truth, and it turns out to be disintegrating and absolute. As Mancini[16] writes,

When abstraction takes over, thinking according to power is established, which is a kind of *unreality* that becomes effective. In fact, power cannot think (*Denken*), it can only dissect (*Zerdenken*) everything with an obsessive reasoning. The impossibility of thinking, for power, derives from the lack of freedom and spiritual subjectivity, from the emptiness constituted by its devastating self-referentiality. It can produce automatic logics that are 'rigorous' because they are oppressive and not because they are authentically rigorous.

In society, this kind of power finds its expression in the triumph of the ideology of technology. Technology responds only to itself. By definition, it is excluding; it gives the word only to those who embody it. In short, technology does not pose ethical problems (if not, hypocritically, "on Sunday").[17] It is not for nothing that politics should always be placed above technology, in order to interpret the demands of all and to balance its one-sidedness. But one of the ways in which a perverse power maintains itself is by pretending to submit to technology. "Pretend" is perhaps not the right word, because it can actually happen, and politics itself is ultimately deprived of technical power.

Let me summarize my argument. Like any institution, psychoanalysis can be alienated as a form of power and a source of suffering. But psychoanalysis also has a great virtue. Using its own tools, it has always engaged in a rigorous process of self-criticism, which represents all its strength intact. This process has taken the form of the theoretical and practical activity of integrating more and more into the field of observation the conscious and unconscious subjectivity of the observer, as a way of rediscovering each time the relationship of equality that underlies mutual recognition. Psychoanalysis has therefore always been devoted to a form of self-cure—for example, by postulating the need for the formative analysis of the analyst, his or her ongoing self-analysis, and supervision.

Psychoanalysis not only provides us with metapsychological and empirical hypotheses as to how these forms of alienation, from which it itself may suffer, arise in the subject and in the social subject from splitting as a defense against distress, which then manifests itself as arrogance, but it can also provide a model of self-understanding for other institutions. Indeed, psychoanalysis theorizes the necessity (or rather, recognizes the inevitability) of the relationship becoming "sick" as an indispensable step toward "healing", so that the whole process has an experiential rather than an intellectual depth.

Throughout his work, Freud often left luminous footnotes, like "little letters", on themes that he did not have time to develop, but which he has left us as a legacy. In our case, too, it is symbolically necessary to start again from the footnote in *Civilization and Its Discontents* where he mentions the meaning of the "experience of being loved [*Liebeserfahrung*]". In this context Freud does so in order to indicate the role of the environment in determining psychic trauma; at the same time, however, it is as if were inscribing the whole experience[18] of analysis within the same framework. Knowledge not as an end in itself, neither in treatment nor in society, which would be the expression of a nefarious "secessionist abstraction".[19] Knowledge, on the other hand, as a means to achieve relations of equality and reconciliation. We can see how close the connection is between our concepts of truth and ethical life.

Notes

1   Roth, *The Human Stain* (Boston/New York: Houghton Mifflin Company, 2000); *The Plot Against America* (Boston & New York: Houghton Mifflin Company, 2004).

2   But see L. Zoja, *Storia dell'arroganza. Psicologia e limiti dello sviluppo* (Bergamo: Moretti&Vitali, 2010); besides, cf. S. Akhtar and A. Smolen, *Arrogance: Developmental, Cultural, and Clinical Realms* (London: Routledge, 2018).

3   M. Heidegger, *The Concept of Time* [1924], transl. W. McNeill (Oxford, UK: Blackwell, 1992), 14E.

4   Cf. D. D'Alessandro, ed., *Filosofia e psicanalisi. Le parole e i soggetti* (Udine-Milano: Mimesis, 2020).

5   Cf. A. Ferro and G. Civitarese, *The Analytic Field and its Transformations*. (London: Routledge, 2014).

6   J. Derrida, *The Gift of Death* [1992], transl. di D. Willis (Chicago & London: The University of Chicago Press, 1995), 25.

7   S. Freud, "Civilization and its Discontents." *The Standard Edition of the Complete Psychological Works of Sigmund Freud* 21 (1930): 57–146.

8   Cf. R. Mancini, *Le logiche del male. Teoria critica e rinascita della società* (Torino: Rosenberg & Sellier, 2012), 57: "The readings offered by Fromm, Neumann, and Ricoeur allow us to understand in what sense Freud's reflection can fit into the perspective of a critical theory".

9   R. Barthes, *Roland Barthes by Roland Barthes* [1975], transl. R. Howard (Berkeley & Los Angeles: California University Press, 1994), 47: "The *Doxa* [...] is Public Opinion, the mind of the majority, petit bourgeois Consensus, the Voice of Nature, the Violence of Prejudice. We can call (using Leibnitz's word) a *doxology* any way of speaking adapted to appearance, to opinion, or to practice".

10 Cf. S. Freud, "Group Psychology and the Analysis of the Ego." *The Standard Edition of the Complete Psychological Works of Sigmund Freud* 18 (1921):65–144, 115, where he assimilates the hypnotic relation to "a group formation with two members [*eine Massenbildung zu zweien*]", and speaks of the individual who is a member of the group as a "group individuals [*Massenindividuum*]" (*ibid.*, 117). Cf. also, in the same essay, the passage in which Freud advances the hypothesis that "love relationships (or, to use a more neutral expression, emotional ties) also constitute the essence of the group mind" (91). Lastly, at 69: "The contrast between individual psychology and social or group psychology, which at a first glance may seem to be full of significance, loses a great deal of its sharpness when it is examined more closely." On this, cf. also G. Civitarese, "Experiences in Groups as a key to 'late' Bion", *The International Journal of Psychoanalysis* 102, no. 6 (2021): 1071–1096.

11 Cf. W. R. Bion, *Experiences in Groups and Other Papers* (New York: Brunner-Routledge, 1961), 116–117: "I mean to indicate, by its use, the individual's readiness to enter into combination with the group in making and acting on the basic assumptions […] he can have, in my view, no valency only by ceasing to be, as far as mental function is concerned, human. Although I use this word to describe phenomena that are visible as, or deducible from, psychological events, yet I wish also to use it to indicate a readiness to combine on levels that can hardly be called mental at all but are characterized by behaviour in the human being that is more analogous to tropism in plants than to purposive behaviour such as is implicit in a word like 'assumption'. In short, I wish to use it for events in the *pm* system should need arise." For the concept of "valence", see K. Lewin, *A Dynamic Theory of Personality: Selected Papers*, transl. D. K. Adams (New York: McGraw-Hill, 1935).

12 On this concept, that we owe to J. Grotstein, see G. Civitarese, "The Grid and the Truth Drive." *The Italian Psychoanalytic Annual* 7 (2013): 91–114. By 'truth drive' we may not mean the search for abstract content that would represent 'true' assertions about reality, at least not in the first instance, but rather the individual's drive to attune to the other in order to reach an agreement that is primarily emotional. For Bion, such 'agreement' is the factor that fosters the growth of the psyche. To make a mind, another mind (actually, *several* minds) is necessarily required. Any kind of human truth, even the most abstract, can only be based on this first 'understanding of each other', which presupposes language in at least one of the members of the couple-as-system, but is realized through semiotic or non-verbal channels".

13 S. Freud, "Group Psychology and the Analysis of the Ego." *The Standard Edition of the Complete Psychological Works of Sigmund Freud* 18 (1921): 65–144, 87f.

14 Cf. W. R. Bion, *Trasformations*. (London: Karnac, 1965), 46: "The differentiating factor that I wish to introduce is not between conscious and unconscious, but between finite and infinite."

15 For Freud, repression is a kind of 'minor' splitting or dissociation: the subject resolves an internal conflict by making unconscious a content undesirable to moral consciousness; it is like being a bit Jekyll and a bit Hyde, but who still function as 'whole' personalities. For Klein, on the other hand, splitting, unlike dissociation, is less benign because it involves a more minute fragmentation of the personality. On this issue, cf. W. R. Bion, "On Hallucination." *International Journal of Psychoanalysis* 39 (1958): 341–349.

16 R. Mancini, *La fragilità dello Spirito. Leggere Hegel per comprendere il mondo globale* (Milano: FrancoAngeli, 2019), 45.

17 Cf. M. Heidegger, *Leitgedanken zur Entstehung der Metaphysik, der neuzeitlichen Wissenschaft und der modernen Technik* (2009; Vittorio Klostermann: Frankfurt am Main, 2014), 125: "Die Technik läßt sich durch kein Menschentum meistern, weil sie selbst nur vollziehbar wird, wenn ein Menschentum zuvor sich ihr unbedingt unterworfen hat [Technique does not allow itself to be

dominated by any humanity, since it becomes executable only if a humanity has first submitted unconditionally to it]."

18 Cf. M. Heidegger, *On the Way to Language*, transl. D. Hertz. (1959; New York: Harper&Row, 1982), 57: "To undergo an experience with something—be it a thing, a person, or a god—means that this something befalls us, strikes us, comes over us, overwhelms and transforms us. When we talk of "undergoing" an experience, we mean specifically that the experience is not of our own making: to undergo here means that we endure it, suffer it, receive it as it strikes us and submit to it. It is this something itself that comes about, comes to pass, happens." S. Petrosino, *Lo spirito della casa. Ospitalità, intimità e giustizia* (Genova: il melangolo, 2019), 29–30, comments: "Experience is therefore always something unexpected that escapes decision, it is always the result of a *novum* that invests the subject, making him leave an already known to open him up to another knowledge. [...] In the idea of experience, therefore, there is a reference to a movement of exit (the prefix *ex-* emphasises this externalisation) from a limit."

19 R. Mancini, *La fragilità dello Spirito. Leggere Hegel per comprendere il mondo globale*, 167.

Chapter 1

The Characteristics of Arrogance

1.1 Preliminary Definition

What is arrogance? Let's start by saying what it is not. Strictly speaking, it is not violence, nor is it pride or (open) insolence. It can be accompanied by brashness, impudence, haughtiness, foolishness, stupidity, imperiousness, narrow-mindedness, shamelessness, uselessness, and ignorance. The arrogant can not only be overbearing, harsh, defiant, sour, irritable, insolent, boastful, intrusive, and rude but also out of proportion, cruel, disrespectful, presumptuous, insulting, callous, quarrelsome, intemperate, foolish, bullying, boastful, and uncivilized. This parade of vocabulary companions is astonishing when we consider how often we witness the exhibition and even the praise of arrogance.

In Pianigiani's[1] etymological dictionary, we read that arrogant is someone who "at all costs wants more esteem, more stuff, more rights for himself than he deserves; therefore Pretentious, Presumptuous". The arrogant person wants to make his superiority felt. "To arrogate" means "to attribute something unduly to oneself", and obviously comes from *rogare*, that is "to ask", "to demand". The prefix "ad", on the other hand, indicates that the appeal is always addressed to the other, thus emphasizing the strictly relational and interpersonal nature of arrogance. More than a simple appeal, arrogance consists in the resentful and aggressive claim of a good that has been denied or taken away and that is felt to be inherent in the vitality of the individual, in his capacity to exist. This "good" has more to do with *being* than with *having*. Those who lack it feel unduly neglected. The painful need to exist in the eyes of others leads the arrogant person to carry out a double movement, ideally along the same vertical axis but in opposite directions. The possibility for the person to make himself visible is given in the externality of the constricting figure, whereby he can only rise if simultaneously another is lowered.

DOI: 10.4324/9781032669427-2

All of these definitions are interesting. Would it have occurred to us that what distinguishes an arrogant person is this triple ... *more* ... *more* ... *more* demands on others? Instinctively, we would be more inclined to think that the arrogant person does not need to ask; that he should already have this *more* ... *more* ... *more*. The reversal of perspective that the reference to etymology allows us to make is productive. We intuit that the arrogant person is not rich, as might be the case with someone who is proud of what he has inherited or won. The arrogant person is poor. But if he is poor, his poverty is not immediately apparent. In fact, the arrogant person usually arouses reactions of hostility, indignation, and impatience in those with whom he comes into contact and whom he invests with his claim. In those who are not directly affected, however, he can easily arouse a movement of identification. Let's hear what Aristotle[2] says:

> The person who gives insult also belittles; for insult is doing and speaking in which there is shame to the sufferer, not that some advantage may accrue to the doer or because something has happened but for the pleasure of it; for those reacting to something do not give insult but are retaliating. [....] The cause of pleasure to those who give insult is that they think they themselves become more superior by ill-treating others.

In a few words, the Stagirite fixes once and for all the essential characteristics of arrogance, specifying that it has to do with shame, and in particular with forcing the other to feel shame. Since this other, who is humiliated, is the designated victim of arrogance, a sadomasochistic relationship is established between the two. It is purely psychological. It has nothing to do with the order of what is useful, nor with the consummation of revenge ("those reacting to something"), but with pleasure. Pleasure is not sexual pleasure, but the pleasure of feeling superior; in essence, the pleasure of feeling in possession of the ability to act freely in a given context (as they say, of *agency*).

The arrogant person is constantly communicating to the other "you and I are different; more precisely, you are inferior to me". It is a kind of idiosyncratic axiom, an Archimedean point from which the arrogant person frames the world, the lever he "automatically" uses to elevate himself. There is omnipotence, but arrogance is not necessarily omnipotence. You can be omnipotent, behave like Superman or Buzz Lightyear, and not be arrogant at all.

In the seventeenth canto of *Purgatory,* vv. 115–7, Dante[3] expresses the concept as well as it could not be better: the arrogant "There are, who, by abasement of their neighbor,/Hope to excel, and therefore only long/That from his greatness he may be cast down". The arrogant man thus gains the visibility he longed for. He does not realize that he is his own forger. In psychoanalytic terms, arrogance could be seen as a projective micro-identification, i.e., the unconscious fantasy of getting rid of a painful affection by placing it in the other and actively exerting some interpersonal pressure to make the "transfer" successful.

The arrogant of style is the one who looks down on people on the basis of an "aesthetic" principle, for an elitism that is accepted as a rule of life. He is, so to speak, the anti-Whitman. On the other hand, the great American poet says of himself: "Walt Whitman am I, a Kosmos, of mighty Manhattan the son,/Turbulent, fleshy and sensual, eating, drinking and breeding;/No sentimentalist—no stander above men and women, or apart from them".[4]

Here, for the arrogant, "Kosmos" stops at the boundaries of the self. It is the hardening as a mental habit and instinctive reaction to the encounter with the different. It goes without saying that the malignant degeneration of arrogance is racism.[5] Northern Europeans are often arrogant toward Italians, northern Italians toward southern Italians, and all of them together toward non-European immigrants who push at the borders.

As Giambattista Roberti[6] wrote, "the annoyance of some French people is so arrogant that when they arrive in Italy and taste some of our dishes cooked in a different way from that used on the other side of their Alps, they say frankly, even though they are poor men, like masters of dance or language, that it is a disgusting dish" (but in the critical note one can also see a certain reciprocal arrogance in the "poor men"). During the COVID-19 pandemic, some Dutch people competed in expressing arrogant judgments about Italians. Ignoring the tragedy that was unfolding, an English doctor and television presenter declared that the coronavirus was just the umpteenth excuse for Italians to prolong their siesta.

The relationship between arrogance and pride is particularly close, even if the former is usually judged more harshly: "Superbia fa l'om essere arrogante" ("Pride makes a man arrogant") recites a poem by Antonio Beccari.[7] Arrogance is not necessarily impertinent or insolent, it can also "demand the undue with quiet obstinacy",[8] just as abstaining from arrogance can be a refined form of it. "There are some who are arrogant in manners, but for other reasons than arrogance: and there are some who are prudent arrogant, who know how to refrain from reckless arrogance".[9] In itself, not only pride but also abundance can be "a harbinger of arrogance".[10] As Nietzsche[11] observes, "there is arrogance in cordiality, in showing honor, in kindly fa-miliarity, in caressing, in friendly counsel, in acknowledgment of faults, in sympathy for others". Sometimes, I would add to his list, due to the com-plete agenesis of the faculty of self-criticism, arrogance can be displayed even in total good faith.

An arrogant person has a compulsion, which has now become a personality trait, to systematically orchestrate a relational situation in which he or she adopts a bullying attitude toward subordinates. For example, Dr Robert Romano from the television series *ER*. However, this should not be seen as a drive to assert some sort of primal instinct to overpower the other. On the contrary, Dr Romano suffers from a desperate sense of lone-liness. His fragility is so great that in the rare moments when he exposes himself and really puts himself on the line emotionally, one senses that disaster is just around the corner. The castle of the brilliant surgeon, unsur-prisingly nicknamed Rocket, would collapse if it were only for the trivial refusal of a colleague to go out for a beer. Even when he doesn't want to, the arrogant man achieves the opposite of what he wants: he keeps the others at bay. Romano surrounds himself with a kind of magical shield of unpleasantness. Certainly, he also expresses a certain satisfaction with the intimate resentment of not feeling loved. More importantly, he is making a conspicuous plea for help.

Could Romano signal his pain any better? Apparently not. This is why seeing the other person's behavior as a malignant impulse to be condemned is not at all the same as seeing the same behavior as the role assigned to an actor in a play. In the various episodes of the series, his humanity is occa-sionally revealed, and then we are confronted with a person whom we seem never to have really understood. An essentially tragic character, as tragic as his fate. First, he is punished by the gods because the blade of a helicopter cuts off his arm, then he dies in the crash of another helicopter. Like Icarus, but twice unable to even get off the ground with the modern wings of the aircraft that serve the County Hospital of Chicago, less efficient in his ef-forts to rise above others, Dr Romano ends up catastrophically ruined.

In fact, it is counterintuitive to think of the many arrogant characters who tread the public and private stage not as people who cause pain, but as peo-ple who suffer. Yet they belong to both categories. People who suffer and make others suffer is the psychiatric definition of sociopathic personalities. Arrogance—as a way of feeling and behaving that no one can claim to be completely alien to—is a kind of sociopathy in its zero degree.

In fact, what this definition captures at a grossly descriptive level could be extended to any form of psychic suffering. Freud has accustomed us to think that if you suffer from obsessive or hysterical neurosis, of course, there must have been some trauma in the past; that at some stage in the individual's psychosexual development one particular fixation mechanism and not another must have been triggered; but in the end, we no longer see the trauma, we only see this psychological explanation. We no longer see the sociopathy that is at the heart of every psychological pathology. This happens because Freud ends up dealing with the isolated individual, studying him with the attitude of a neurologist. At the same time, the traumatic origin is distanced in time and we struggle to realize that the scene repeats itself incessantly. Or rather, we feel it—the notion of the compulsion to repeat is one of the central notions of psychoanalysis—but we explain it away in terms of the patient's tendency not to understand and to misunderstand; not, perhaps, in terms of the insensitivity of others toward him.

In short, it is difficult to talk about arrogance without falling into a judgmental, moralistic, or pedagogical vision, just by saying things with a certain obvious and everyday lexicon. In doing so, however, we condemn ourselves to not understanding. If, on the other hand, we recognize that at the root of it all is a sense of fear,[12] we have a better chance of not being afraid ourselves, of empathizing with the well-hidden suffering of the other, and also of devising something to "mitigate" the arrogance of the current culture with a kind of education in kindness and hospitality. If the concept of arrogance includes the idea of something overbearing, excessive, obnoxious, unseemly, even, for example, the infamous "You don't know who I am" immortalized in the films of Alberto Sordi, then, for once, it doesn't provoke annoyance but pity. It has the same tragic irony of Oedipus: it is obvious that even the one who utters the fateful phrase does not know who he really is. One might even reply: "Ah! …why, you really think you know who you are?!?".

1.2   Mr Charlus Smiles

The aristocratic and cultured Palamède de Guermantes, Baron de Charlus, whom his sister-in-law sometimes ironically calls Taquin le Superbe, is one of the most fascinating and enigmatic characters in Proust's *Remembrance of Things Past*. Unpredictable in his behavior, erratic in his moods, and unfaithful in love, Mr de Charlus is characterized by boundless pride. At times he can be not only ungrateful, but also mean and even cruel. In one of the key scenes of the novel, the narrator catches him being whipped, revealing not only his sadistic traits but also his deeply masochistic character:

> Then I noticed that this room had a small, round window opening in the hallway, over which they had neglected to draw the curtain; tiptoeing in the darkness, I made my way softly to this window and there, Chained to a bed lie Prometheus to his rock, and being beaten by Maurice with a cat-o-nine-tails which was, as a matter of fact, studded with nails, I saw before me M. de Charlus, bleeding all over and covered with welts which shewed that this was not the first time the torture had taken place.[13]

In some way, this is accompanied by another small but significant epiphany, in which the narrator is also involved in the first person. The two "pictures" are like the warp and weft of the same fabric because they show the necessary interweaving of love and hate.

> These general features of a whole family took on, however, in the face of M. de Charlus a fineness more spiritualized, above all more gentle. I regretted for his sake that he should habitually adulterate with so many acts of violence, offensive oddities, tale-bearings, with such harshness, susceptibility and arrogance, that he should conceal beneath a false brutality the amenity, the kindness which, at the moment of his emerging from Mme. de Villeparisis's, I could see displayed so innocently upon his face. Blinking his eyes in the sunlight, he seemed almost to be smiling, I found in his face seen thus in repose and, so to speak, in its natural state something so affectionate, so disarmed, that I could not help thinking how angry M. de Charlus would have been could he have known that he was being watched; for what was suggested to me by sight of this man who was so insistent, who prided himself so upon his virility, to whom all other men seemed odiously effeminate, what he made me suddenly think of, so far had he momentarily assumed her features, expression, smile, was a woman.[14]

Proust's extraordinary sensitivity gives his observations a quasi-psychoanalytic or theoretical quality. Charlus consciously hides his sexual "inversion" under a mask of hypervirility. In doing so, he respects the norms of the family (the "general features") and society. The narrator regrets that

Charlus is forced to wear a mask of brutality and arrogance, because it prevents his most authentic human qualities from appearing. There is, however, a double irony in his sadness. To surprise Charlus at a moment when he has lowered his defenses, when he feels the sun's rays caressing his face and revealing his most intimate being, the author is also a homosexual and a member of the Sodom and Gomorrah which gives the volume its title. Proust identifies himself with the character of the narrator, who has his own name but is not homosexual. The author, therefore, also "hides". A double "reversal" of perspective is thus achieved. The element that Charlus wants to deny, i.e., homosexuality, is confirmed twice. First, it is literally revealed ("he was a woman"); secondly, the ray of light that strikes him comes from the gaze of someone who shares his secret.

The scene shows, however, that if Charlus is very careful about his public image, it is not only because of the obvious need for secrecy. It is because he unconsciously feels transparent in the eyes of others. To put it in Freudian[15] terms, he knows that he has not paid for his ticket, or that he has only paid for half of it. The torment he suffers internally is the same as the narrator's when, at the beginning of the *Recherche*, he recalls the pain he felt as a child on the evenings when, because Swann was visiting, his mother did not come up to kiss him goodnight.

In his list of Charlus's negative traits, Proust links "susceptibility" to "arrogance" with an "and", as if the two terms formed a particularly significant syntactic unit. He does not, for example, write, as he might have done, arrogance *and* "violence" or arrogance *and* offensive "oddities". The conjunction thus takes on the significance of a brilliant insight. It is as if it binds the two concepts in a relationship of a genetic nature. Charlus is *susceptible*, which means that it takes little to affect his emotional makeup in a negative way, that is, to hurt and offend him. Otherwise, he would not need to wear the armor which, in the current moment described here, in which he does not feel observed, he can finally lay down. The sweet warmth of the sun's rays on his face, and the smile that he finally turns toward himself (and toward life), comes from the recognition that has taken place without his knowledge, and which the episode brilliantly allegorizes. But any recognition is rooted in an intersection of glances, a seeing each other[16] that only partly takes place in the clarity of explicit intentions and verbal communication. In Charlus, the narrator sees a woman's smile, but at the same time, it is as if Charlus himself, through the narrator, sees himself[17] in his mother's eyes and smiling face, and thus identifies with her. It doesn't matter that Charlus is unaware of this. The scene reveals the phantasmatic foundation on which each individual's ego and sense of self are based.

There is another aspect I would like to emphasize. The vision that Proust makes us witness here is also a transgression; in Freudian terms, a "primary scene" situation: the equivalent of observing the mother in her moment of intimacy, as depicted allegorically in so many paintings that have as their subject, for example, the biblical Susanna caught in the bath by two old men. On the one hand, this overstepping of boundaries is a ubiquitous unconscious fantasy; on the other hand, in this context, an accidental situation that has arisen suggests that if Charlus, when he is not alone, generally has to falsify his true self, to assume a pose, it is because he himself has often suffered painful violations of his own psychic space. Just as in the first scene, that of sexual perversion, the sadistic side reveals the masochistic one, so in the second, which shows Charlus leaving Madame de Villeparisis's house, arrogance gives way to tenderness, leaving us to guess at the lack that is at the root of it all.

The homosexuality of both Charlus and Proust (along with the clandestine nature of the narrator's vision and the voyeuristic impulse of any reader/spectator), rather than referring to the specific subject matter, serves in the quotation to allude to the nature of psychic life in general, and how much one inexorably remains "secret" even to oneself. As if to remind us that we all live in the invisible dimension of the unconscious, of multiple and automatic identifications. In the note that accompanies the Italian translation, the editors note how often terms such as "nature", "natural", "naturally" recur in these pages, as if the author wanted to emphasize his way of looking at homosexuality. But it could be read in a broader sense: as an affirmation that our nature is not to be masters of ourselves.

This is only the last game of mirrors, the most veiled. The reader is reflected in Marcel, *alias* the narrator, who in turn identifies with Charlus. The noble character is sad *about himself* and the feelings of anger ("how angry M. de Charlus would have been") and hatred ("odiously") for the object that, as Freud[18] beautifully writes, unconsciously falls like a shadow on the ego. *What this passage tells us is that any form of arrogance is but the visible part of this invisible cone of shadow.* But it also tells us that some form of redemption is possible. The whole episode could be seen as a paradigm of aesthetic experience, as an experience of unity with the object (or its spirit), which is common to all those who participate in the scene from different points of view, and of the happy containment of fear.

If instead we return for a moment to the scene of sexual perversion, the obligatory reference is Freud's essay "A Child is Being Beaten".[19] On the basis of what we think of masochism today, i.e., that it is difficult to attribute it, as Freud ultimately does, to the inexorable action of the death instinct, we would say that even the arrogant person is constantly engaged in repeating a sadomasochistic scene. The unconscious aim would be to metaphorize one episode with another by going through an innumerable series of set-ups and rehearsals. In this way, he hopes to arrive at a "concept" of it and thus finally be able to master the trauma that triggered the process.

1.3   Susceptibility of Henry V

In literature, one of the most famous manifestations of arrogance is to be found in Shakespeare's *Henry V*. The young king has claimed a number of possessions in France. The Dauphin (not even the King himself) instructs ambassadors to convey to him his refusal to give in to his demands. But he does not stop there. He crosses the line and, taking advantage of the familiarity that comes from being cousins, has them deliver a gift.

This is the real opening scene of the drama, the moment when a violent passion is ignited, which we will see flare up and extinguish (significantly) when, according to a psychoanalytical reading of the events, the hero will be able to regain contact with a feminine that can only symbolically stand for the maternal object:

KING HENRY
[...]
Therefore with frank and with uncurbèd plainness
Tell us the Dauphin's mind.

AMBASSADOR
Thus, then, in few:
Your Highness, lately sending into France,
Did claim some certain dukedoms in the right
Of your great predecessor, King Edward the Third;
In answer of which claim, the Prince our master
Says that you savor too much of your youth
And bids you be advised there's naught in France
That can be with a nimble galliard won;

You cannot revel into dukedoms there.
He therefore sends you, meeter for your spirit,
This tun of treasure and, in lieu of this,
Desires you let the dukedoms that you claim
Hear no more of you. This the Dauphin speaks.

KING HENRY
What treasure, uncle?

EXETER Tennis balls,
my liege.[20]

Giving tennis balls to a king sounds like an intolerable insult. In a gesture of defiance, the Dauphin intends to put Henry in a position of inferiority. He does not recognize his rank. Indeed, he refers several times to his youth and inexperience. Nor does Shakespeare fail to underline the pleasure the Frenchman takes in mocking his opponent ("Now are we well prepared to know the pleasure/Of our fair cousin Dauphin").[21] The ambassador points out that his predecessor was indeed a great king.

Henry's reply is one of the most extraordinary monologues in the Shakespearean theatre. The tirade is articulated in such an overwhelming crescendo that it makes you shiver and vividly anticipates the power and fury with which the young king will punish France. In particular, the repetition of the verb to mock is a rhetorical device that fulfills a precise function in the text: it expresses Henry's explosion of rage in two different scenarios, one actual and the other foreshadowed, linked by a cause–effect relationship. Its purpose is to emphasize the humiliation suffered at the hands of the Dauphin's arrogance and to reverse it in the thunder of the obsessive blows with which he will destroy him.

KING HENRY
[…]
And tell the pleasant prince this mock of his
Hath turned his balls to gun-stones, and his soul
Shall stand sore chargèd for the wasteful vengeance
That shall fly with them; for many a thousand widows
Shall this his mock mock out of their dear husbands,
Mock mothers from their sons, mock castles down;

And some are yet ungotten and unborn
That shall have cause to curse the Dauphin's scorn.[22]

In a later scene, Exeter, as Henry's ambassador, returns to the scene of the mockery and reports to the Dauphin.

EXETER
[...]
Thus says my king: an if your father's Highness
Do not, in grant of all demands at large,
Sweeten the bitter mock you sent his Majesty,
He'll call you to so hot an answer of it
That caves and womby vaultages of France
Shall chide your trespass and return your mock
In second accent of his ordinance.[23]

Of course, the adjective "womby" mocks this very threat. Indeed, it alludes to what will happen to the women of France once they have been conquered. Let us also bear in mind the reference to those who are "yet ungotten and unborn". Remember that in Greek "rape" is said ὕβρίς[24] and ὑβρίζειν is the corresponding verb. Thus, Henry's revenge on those who have treated him arrogantly (but also disproportionate is his claim to take possession of something that does not belong to him, and so is the absolute conviction that he is right to take revenge) culminates again in the unconscious fantasy of rejoining the maternal, a maternal even more primitive than that which can be read in the watermark in the scene of Charlus (the feminine smile). It is the never-ending desire to return to the first safe place, the mother's womb.[25] Conversely, this same fantasy leads us to reflect on the factor that lies at the origin of arrogance: the feeling of anger at the unconscious experience of being prematurely and violently expelled from the womb.

1.4   The Women of Agamemnon

The first time we read in the *Iliad* the word *hýbris* is in verse 204 of Book I. The context is a meeting of the Greeks to decide on the return of Chryseides, enslaved by Agamemnon, to her father Chryse, priest of Apollo. The leader of the great expedition against the Trojans proved to be arrogant, demanding in return "Brisèis[26], daintily featured", the slave of Achilles. Only the providential intervention of Athena calms the fury of Achilles, who is ready to draw his sword against Agamemnon. The goddess is furious: "her eyes shone fearfully on him", writes Homer.[27] Achilles is astonished to see Athena, but he immediately recognizes her and addresses her: "Why thus here upon Earth?.../Is it, that thou may'st note the injurious pride [ὕβριν] of Atrides?/Then, do thou hear me predict—and see the prediction accomplished—/Soon shall his forfeit life pay the price of his insolent rashness [ὑπεροπλίῃσι]!".[28] Achilles does not know it, but this is exactly what will happen, though not as he imagines. We note that, at the very moment when Agamemnon's death is evoked, there is an interesting attenuation from ὕβριν to ὑπεροπλίῃσι, as if to allude to the resizing of guilt that follows the atonement for sin.

Against Agamemnon then stands the son of Peleus. More than an invective, it is a diagnosis:

"Dog as thou art in face; tame at heart as the deer of the woodlands;/ Sot of a king!—When wert thou ever seen, mid the lords of Achaia,/ Arm'd in the van of fight; or, in the more perilous ambush,/Winning the spoils of a foe?—Not for thee such uncertain encounters!"[29]. Achilles therefore paints Agamemnon as a coward. The consequences for the Greeks will be disastrous, he threatens: "When in their utmost need, when all the sons of Achaia,/Yearn for Achilleus' help—they may yearn for, but shall not obtain it!/Then when, unequal to aid, thou beholdest the heaps of the dying/Piled by the arm of Hector, —the arm of the homicide Hector—/Bitterly then shalt thou rue, in remorse and in anguish of spirit,/Rue that day when thy madness dishonor'd the bravest Achaian"[30]. Achilles, as they say, puts his finger on the sore spot: 'you want to be more than you are'.

Indeed, this is not the first time that the son of Atreus has shown himself to be arrogant. Moreover, the scene of destruction that Achilles projects into the near future has already happened, and Agamemnon doesn't seem to have learned his lesson. When Chryse goes to him to ask for the return of his daughter, who was a victim of the sack of Thebes, Agamemnon insults him and drives him away in a rude manner, arousing the wrath of Apollo. The scene is one of those that are never forgotten: Apollo "and the people/Died in heaps around; and wider still did his arrows/Range thro' the hosts of Achaia".[31]

Agamemnon and Achilles had already met, and the repetition says that the two characters express values that go far beyond their individual lives. In *Iphigenia in Aulis*, Euripides recounts how Agamemnon, without telling him, pretended to give him his daughter in marriage for the sole purpose of luring her to the ritual sacrifice, without either her or her mother suspecting a thing. "Some one hath surely sported with us both",[32] Achilles says to Clytemnestra on this occasion.

But this is not the first time that Agamemnon shows a tragic lack of boundaries. His arrogance is also at the root of the sacrifice of his daughter Iphigenia. In fact, the myth tells us that he killed an animal sacred to Artemis and, in a variant, that he boasted of his superiority in the use of the bow. As you can imagine, Artemis did not take kindly to this and stopped the Greeks' ships until she was satisfied with the offense she had suffered.

Agamemnon's character is also revealed by the invective with which Menelaus, his brother, apostrophizes him when he sees him hesitate to sacrifice Iphigenia so that the Greek fleet can set sail. Menelaus is sarcastic and casts an ominous light on him: "What grief and what confusion did those eyes/Express, as if depriv'd of your command/Over a thousand ships, ere you have cover'd/The fields of Priam with avenging troops!/To me you then applied; 'how shall I act,/'What scheme devise?' lest stripp'd of such high rank,/You with your power should forfeit all renown./Since Calchas at the holy rites declar'd/Your daughter to Diana must be given/In sacrifice, the in these terms, the host/A favourable voyage would await,/With joy you promis'd of your own accord/To offer up the victim".[33] *And so it happens*.

Even when he's forced to repent for his arrogance, Agamemnon calls himself out and blames the Gods for what has happened: "Many's the time and oft I have heard from the sons of Achaia/Words of reproach and blame; but I am not responsible to them./Zeus was in fault; and Fate; and the Fury that wanders in darkness./These are the powers that cast on my sense the curse of contention;/On that day when I ventured to plunder the prize of Achilleus./How could I otherwise act?—'Twas the God who thus work'd to his own/ends".[34] Achilles has a different opinion on how things stand, but curiously anticipates his rival's self-absolution ('he is insane'): "Once he has wrong'd and deceived me.—Again, he in vain may attempt it,/Smoothing me over with words.—One success is enough.—Let him perish/Unregarded—a wretch whom Zeus has deprived of his reason".[35]

As Calasso[36] points out, "Agamemnon carries out the law of men [...] with a watchful eye on the multitude who obey him". If we consider that at the end of the war the scene is repeated with the sacrifice of Polyxena, Priam's daughter, this time to appease the return of the Achaean ships to their homeland, and that she was to have married Achilles (*sic*), who had fallen in love with her, we can see that both Greek heroes are trapped in the forced repetition of the same pattern. When they enter the scene, they represent "two one-sidedness" that could be reconciled, as in the case of Odysseus, but do not. On the one hand the law of man, on the other the law of God. The uniqueness of Achilles is that he is the son of a goddess, Thetis. His strength, but also his inhuman cruelty in war, is determined at the moment of his birth, when Thetis throws him into the sea. Except for the heel, the disproportion between the tiny part of the body that remains "human" and therefore vulnerable, and the rest of the body, which is divine and therefore knows no wound, alludes to the imbalance or radical division that marks his character.

So there are four women in Agamemnon's way: Iphigenia, Briseis, Polyxena, and Chryseides. We know that when he returns home at the end of the war, the fifth, his bride Clytemnestra, will settle all his scores in one fell swoop. Finally, the Agamemnon-Achilles couple is an echo of the man-woman couple. It is as if Achilles, the most masculine of men (from this point of view, his divine side is a hyperbole), expressed the great power of the feminine, the same implacability and embodiment of the absolute that makes Clytemnestra, Medea, and Antigone sublime. Perhaps it is a detail not to be overlooked that Achilles had the privilege of growing up among little girls.

The fact that these pairs of characters are created is a sign that the problem is never to be found on one side or the other, but rather in the caesura that unites them by separating them and, at the same time, makes them individuals by uniting them. The problem is not the caesura as such, but the fact that when the opposition becomes rigid, the caesura can no longer be transcended,[37] it can no longer be dialectized.

1.5 Blindness of Antigone

In Section A of Chapter VI of *The Phenomenology of Spirit*, Hegel[38] tells the story of how the subject becomes such, that is, acquires self-consciousness, through mutual recognition. At the center of a splendid but impervious prose, he embeds three fictional narratives—literature thus enriches speculative thought with all the integrative power of its imagination and art of expression. It is the allegory of the struggle between master and servant; then, taken from Sophocles, of the conflict between Creon and Antigone; and finally, from Diderot's *Rameau's Nephew*, that between Bertin and Rameau. These are the pages in which the text "dreams", that is to say, it produces extraordinarily and creatively ambiguous images, and in so doing, in a way, shows what it is about, something related to a certain idea of infinity, and which, in principle, no reason can ever contain exhaustively.

In the dense and compact web of language that Hegel invents to undertake his dizzying journey into the meanders of the history of the mind, these stories of fiction stand out like so many hyperluminous images. Like those memories which Freud[39] explains that if they are *überdeutlich*, that is, "ultra-clear", it is because they refer to something traumatic. They are the places to which one returns again and again, questioning them in the hope of eventually integrating them into the dense fabric of memory—in our case, of grasping the sense of the intersubjective dynamic that generates what is human, and also of a certain inevitable violence inherent in the process.

What is astonishing to us is that all the figures evoked have to do with arrogance. In each case, Hegel presents arrogance as a stage in a process that leads, after various vicissitudes, to mutual recognition (*Anerkennung*) or reconciliation (*Versöhnung*);[40] but also, when the dynamic crystallizes, to splitting (*Entzweiung*) as its antithesis and failure. And these are all negative examples. There is no reconciliation between Antigone and Creon, or between Rameau and Bertin. In particular, Antigone, which Hegel[41] considers to be "the most magnificent and satisfying work of art of this kind" of all the masterpieces of classical antiquity, stands out as a memorable and dramatic representation of the alienation resulting from the struggle between two different and opposing forms of "one-sidedness of a 'pathos'"[42] or arrogance.

We are at the scene[43] where, for the first time, two very strong wills collide in a direct way.

CHORUS

A raw response that shows the father's mood:
Ever head-on, no bending to the blast

CREON

Hear me! Observe, I say! I'd have you know
That stubborn brows are those that meet the dust.
The stiffest iron, hardened in the forge,
Splinters and snaps in use. Do we not see
The foaming courseners in his air plunge
Gentled and broken by a tiny curb?
Thy self-importance ill becomes a slave.
                    (To the Chorus)
She ever had a trick of insolence
Or e'er she trampled on my last decree.
This outrage is but sequel to the rest:—
She boasts of it and glories in her deed.
Am I the man, or is this girl the man,
To win the bout and walk un scathed away?
No! Be she sister's child, or closer blood
Than all that clusters of our family
Round Zeus' inmost altar, neither she,
No, nor her sister—whom I also charge
As co-conspirator—shall 'scape the doom
For their connivance in this burial.

The "stubborn brows", that is, the will or characters (φρονήματα) that are too "hard" (σκλήρ, which also means "obstinate", "cruel"), are like the "hard" (ἐγκρατέστατον) iron that fire has "hardened" (περισκελῆ, a term also used as "inflexible", "harsh", "severe"). The repetition involved in moving from σκλήρ to περισκελῆ has the effect of intensifying harshness and transmuting it into the arrogance of φρονεῖν μέγα. It is a short step from here to pride becoming an insult, an act expressed by the verb ὑβρίζειν, the step is short. That this is an excess of pride is clear from the hammering compulsion to repeat that after ὑβρίζειν makes Creon utter the verb ὑπερβαίνουσα ("trampling on the laws", i.e., "transgressing"), then the noun ὕβρις, rendered here as "contempt" (but it could also be "insult").

In order to convey the crescendo of rage that invades Creon, an effect that in itself "interprets" the boundless arrogance of Antigone, but ironically also of the king himself, Sophocles describes Antigone as not satiated by the offense already given, irreconcilable and implacable: "This outrage is but sequel to the rest". She cannot resist adding a second insult to the first (ΰβρις). Having done what she has done, she even "laughs" at it. The word ἀνατὶ (impunity), uttered at this point by Creon, makes it clear, if it were ever needed, that in his eyes Antigone is making a mockery of the laws.

"Thy self-importance ill becomes a slave", says Creon. Now, on the one hand, we are all "slaves" to others, that is, we are "physiologically" dependent on each other; on the other hand, true slavery occurs when the necessary alienation through which the self-constitutes itself by welcoming the other is degraded to colonizing. We do not know whether Hegel was inspired by these lines when he wrote about the dialectic of recognition using the allegory of the relationship between master and servant. The hypothesis is suggestive, however, also because the second impressive allegory of the *Phenomenology* concerns Antigone.

The two contenders both think that the basis of law to which each refers is *immediate*, that is, not mediated, "ontological", absolute. As such, it would be a datum not of culture but of nature. This is the emotional attitude not only of Antigone but also of Creon. Although he knows on a factual level that the laws of the State are human, he nevertheless derives them from a divine principle.[44] Since this split logic remains between the two positions, it is clear that there is no space for possible integration. What separates them is the dramatic cut of a non-dialectical and non-solidaristic antagonism between the conscience of the community and the conscience of the individual.

Creon, then, is therefore for what is human, explicit, conscious, genetic, historical, of the order of *becoming*; Antigone for what is divine, unconscious, static, immutable, of the order of *being*. The laws invoked by Creon clear, written, the result of community deliberation; those invoked by Antigone are obscure, unwritten, transcending the individual. From a psychoanalytic point of view, Creon and Antigone can be seen, respectively, as the spokesmen of the two polarities that normally correlate dialectically to constitute the subject: the conscious polarity, subjective or finite, and the unconscious one, intersubjective or infinite.[45]

More exactly, what they allegorize is the split that occurs when the movement of uplifting transformation or overcoming conflict (*Aufhebung*) is broken, which in this case would be represented by the event of mutual recognition. Mutual recognition is the needle that knots in the subject conscious and unconscious, norm of the State and norm of the family (or blood), but also particular and universal. In essence, it is the work of the concept or of the abstract, which in the primary relationship between mother and child can only be achieved on the level of feelings and affections, initially passive and anonymous and only later claimed by consciousness. The work of this needle, which in psychoanalysis coincides with the moment of becoming one (at-one-ment), of the "dyadic expansion of consciousness",[46] of *being one*—an event that obeys the logic of symmetrization of love[47] and not the hierarchical logic of power and abstract possession in the form of knowledge—is interrupted when the relationship produces a paranoid stiffening triggered by fear.

When the needle stops knotting its threads, and the abstract logic stops listening to the reasons of the emotional body, the subject no longer understands the why of things, he is unsettled. He loses the compass that gives him a reliable account at all times of what is or is not valid in his experience of the world. Not only that. Lacking the organizing tension of the elastic band of emotion, that runs through them internally, the thoughts themselves, though they may still appear to be connected (but sometimes, as in schizophrenia, they cease to be) seem as if they go round in circles. They no longer stand upright. Awareness of the emotional life is lost and so life is as if invaded and suspended.[48]

It is the same drama of Oedipus, who in the name of the will to know and the concern for the government and the common good, despises the divine truth of which Tiresias becomes the interpreter. For Oedipus, the reconciliation takes place on the threshold of death, in *Oedipus at Colonus*, when by now the tragic hero par excellence, as Hegel writes, "with his plasticity of consciousness, takes responsibility for what he has done as an individual and does not cut his purely subjective self-consciousness apart from what is objectively the case. [...] No worse insult could be given to such a hero than to say that he had acted innocently".[49] Here is the point, this would be tantamount to disrespecting the subterranean gods of the unconscious.[50]

Thus, the real *hýbris*, to go beyond the limit, to commit a sacrilege, to be arrogant, is not so much the criminal act itself—as we shall see shortly, this is the shift in meaning that Bion proposes in the interpretation of the Oedipus myth—but rather the failure to take responsibility for it, and thus to reconcile the split between "the two unilateralities" of conscious and unconscious, heaven and earth, intellect and reason. Instead, when such reconciliation takes place, "[Oedipus'] blind eyes are transfigured and clear".[51]

Hegel anticipates the wisdom of Freud and psychoanalysis, and at the same time gives the impression of seeing more clearly on at least one essential point (but it is obvious that we can only read him in this way *after* Freud). Where Freud seems to stop at the recognition by the subject of his aggressive drives directed to the father, and of his erotic drives directed toward the mother, but in a context that remains individualistic, Hegel makes it clear that the split is both vertical, i.e., within the subject, and horizontal, between the subject and the social community.[52] Breaking the continuity between conscious and unconscious or between subjectivity and intersubjectivity is equivalent to establishing a non-permeable caesura, which, as such, when violated, alienates the subject in an act of arrogance. On the other hand, when there is no split, conscious and unconscious function in an integrated way. Each of the two terms denies (limits) the other and at the same time preserves it. This means, as we say, that the ego is the Other; that we are spoken to by the unconscious and by language just as much as we contribute to their expansion. Essentially it means recognizing that truth is based on mediation; that it is never "obvious" or *immediate*.

Antigone, as we have said, defends divine (natural) law against Creon, who embodies human law instead. Creon *knows* what he is doing, he is rational and aware. His edict on Polynices is clear: "that man no tomb/Shall clasp. No voice bewail, but he shall lie/A mangled meal for dogs and birds of prey".[53] Not so Antigone, though tough and determined in her will, for the law of blood is dark.

The irony of the situation is that both somehow express the same truth: Creon, that reality is mediated by interhuman agreement; Antigone, that it is mediated by the "divine" (actually very human) nature of language.[54] What is the difference? Exactly, that in a way Creon knows it and Antigone doesn't, and that's why she thinks there is no mediation instead. One speaks for the conscious, the other for the unconscious.[55] Not only that they constantly exchange cards as the head of the community, Creon represents its right; but as the spokesperson of intersubjectivity as the "common essence" of the subject, Antigone also represents the community, but a much larger, *infinite* community.

As king, Creon places himself above the community he represents and does so on a vertical and asymmetrical axis. As a sister, in fighting for the burial of Polynices, Antigone places herself above her brother on a horizontal and symmetrical axis. I wonder if this is not a possible key to understanding the strange motivation that Antigone gives to Creon to justify her actions: that is, precisely because it is a brother, and not a son or a husband, he must do what he must do. His parents are dead and could never again give her another brother. In fact, there is reciprocity between brothers and sisters. Theirs is not a relationship of dependence, like that between parent and child, nor is it based on desire, like that between mother and father.

But let's see what kind of dizzying game Sophocles has gotten us into? As is obvious, Antigone no longer has any brothers. The two brothers she did have are both dead. Read allegorically, Antigone's claim would correspond to the obscure intuition that at the level of the unconscious there is not and can be no asymmetry; and that it is only at this level that an authentic recognition can take place safe from the falsity of consciousness. If only the absolute symmetry of the unconscious could exist, there would be no body of the brother murdered by the brother. The political community (consciousness) is born precisely from the overcoming of this indifference (of the unconscious), or rather from an overcoming that recognizes and maintains it at some level. One would think that the community of the ego/government (the universal concept and law) would always prevail over individuality (the particular), because without reflective community there would be no self-consciousness, only animality. But the fact is that even the unconscious (not the instinctual) of the individual is made up of language and therefore of community. We must not fall into the temptation of establishing another caesura. There has always been a relationship of co-originality and co-implication between subjectivity and intersubjectivity.[56] Thus, the conflict between the divine law and the law of blood on which Hegel dwells on, must first of all be reinterpreted as a split, internal to the subject, between subjectivity and intersubjectivity.

There is no process of "immunization" between Antigone and Creon. The mutual "infection" of words, ideas, affections, values, which would lead to a strengthening of their identities, is prevented. There is opposition, not dialectic. The fact is that Antigone dies and Creon does not. The end of the tragedy suggests that, although subjectivity and intersubjectivity are both necessary for self-consciousness to exist, the salient element that allows it to be conquered is the ascent to the concept that is made possible by the norms of civilization. But when civilization loses contact with the dark, "bloody" ground from which it emerged, all that remains is the misery of a life that is not a life.

Creon does not die but dies in spirit. Having dodged the sword blow with which his son tries to kill him, he is forced to witness first his own suicide and then that of his wife. The unprecedented violence of the double loss reminds him that the laws of the State are not enough to govern the fate of the human community; that society, we would say with Mancini,[57] cannot be based on power as dominion, but only on truth. As one of my patients put it, "The higher you go, the less life there is; you feel special, but all around you is a desert".

It is as if, when there is a rapture in existence, there are only two ways to go: either to fall into the indistinctness of a hyper-intersubjectivity as the common face of the subject (like falling back into animality), or rise to the heights of a hyper-subjectivity and therefore of abstraction as the negation of life. On the basis of the colonizing power of the intellect on the body, we understand that the second solution is more likely to turn into a request for treatment, whereas the first, which on a clinical level corresponds to an antisocial disorder, if and when is there, comes from the environment.

The struggle between Antigone and Creon thus arises from a split between mind and body, subjectivity and intersubjectivity, knowledge of the intellect, and knowledge of emotions and affections. In an extraordinarily beautiful passage, Hegel[58] describes the relationship between the conscious and the unconscious in the allegorical terms of the state and the family, using the figures of Creon and Antigone as a backdrop. In order to clarify my reading key, in square brackets, I translate the Hegelian figures in the roughly equivalent concepts of psychoanalysis; in particular in the three "instances" (Ego, Id, Super-ego) that Freud gathers in the so-called "second topic", that is in his structural model of the psyche:

> This is a struggle between spirit conscious of itself [*the conscious*] and unconscious spirit [*the* unconscious] [...], for unconscious spirit is the other essential power and is for that reason not destroyed but only offended by the conscious spirit. Yet confronting the authoritative law lying open to the light of day, unconscious spirit [*Id*] has a bloodless shade to help it put its law *actually* into effect. Hence, as the law of weakness and of darkness, it is initially sub-jugated to daylight's law and to its force [*the arrogance of conscience*], for its authority is only valid in the netherworld and not on the earth. However, the actual [*the Ego/agency*], which took its honor and power from the inner [*Id*], has by doing so devoured its essence [*the Ego discovers that it is not master in its own house*]. The revealed spirit [*Ego*] has the roots of its force in the netherworld [*Id*]; the people's self-reassuring *certainty* has the *truth* of its oath which binds them all into one only in the mute unconscious substance of all, in the waters of forgetfulness [*Bion's protomental system/ the intersubjective layer of Being*]. The achievement of public spirit is

thereby transformed into its opposite, and the public spirit experiences that its supreme right is supreme wrong and that its victory is instead its own downfall [*in essence, if one rips out the roots of the ego that sink into the ground of the id, the ego and the id each become in its own way 'supreme' i.e. absolute: at this point ruin is at hand*].

Given the psychopathology of neurosis and psychosis and the way in which these cleavages occur in the primary mother–child relationship, we might venture to say, by analogy, that Antigone and Creon are destined not to understand each other because they are both terribly afraid. They are related to Oedipus and Jocasta. They have lived through a fratricidal war. It is logical that in each of them, these misfortunes raise the superego to a kind of autocracy, and that from the increased pressure exerted by this instance of the psyche comes an increase in paranoid anxiety, a tendency to strict self-control, a drastic restriction of freedom, blind and fanatical obedience to a cruel inner god. As Freud[59] writes, "The field of ethics, which is so full of problems, presents us with another fact: namely that misfortune—that is to say, external frustration—so greatly enhances the power of conscience in the super-ego". Winnicott,[60] on the other hand, would put it this way:

> Some babies, tantalized by this type of relative maternal failure, study the variable maternal visage in an attempt to predict the mother's mood, just exactly as we all study the weather. The baby quickly learns to make a forecast: "Just now it is safe to forget about the mother's mood and be spontaneous, but any minute the mother's face will become fixed or her mood will dominate, and my own personal need must then be withdrawn otherwise my central self may suffer insult.

As we can see, if bad weather threatens, the subject withdraws from the libidinal and affective body and relies primarily on intellectual and abstract defenses. Being dependent on the object, in order to save himself, the child must give up becoming himself. He cannot listen to the sirens of desire, not even by plugging his ears. He cannot have *more* affects, *more* eyes,[61] but can only adhere to *one* point of view. He has the illusion of knowing. He becomes shy and insecure or brash and arrogant. Either way, he lives in fear and in the absolute.

In short, in Creon and Antigone, the same unhealthy impulse of Oedipus to want to know the truth at all costs is reborn; or, which is the same, to pretend that one's own is the only truth, a fact of nature. Antigone and

Creon are arrogant because they do not recognize the conventional, social status of laws. If they did, Creon would see that Antigone's position, too, is legitimately based on a rational order, albeit a rationality that is not abstract and withered. And Antigone would see that ultimately even the written law has its own legitimacy. Both would discover the value of ambiguity. Isn't that why we say that laws have to be interpreted?[62] A reconciliation could only take place if they recognized that both are "human". Not only the former, which seems self-evident, but also the latter, even though they emerge from processes of interhuman negotiation of the meaning of things that take place not only through explicit or verbal channels but also through implicit-non-verbal ones.

If this were the case (but in Sophocles' tragedy, on the "realistic" level of the plot, this is not how things work), then Antigone and Creon would each be obliged to acknowledge that the human is in the divine (but now a divine in inverted commas: the "divine nature" of language[63]) and vice versa, and therefore that each of them is also present in both spirit and the flesh of the other. They would discover that access to the other, and the other to them, coincides, so to speak, with the very process of becoming subjects. The *other* and the *self* would appear to them as different aspects of the same reality. Such an awareness would lead them to consider the needs of the other and to find a point of mediation.

An event like this would always be emblematic of how the journey of civilization itself begins and continues, or, which is the same thing from another point of view, psychic individuation. There would no longer be any place for an "absolute" or immediate position, that is to say, "liberated" from the constraints of the negotiations between people and between them and nature that takes place simultaneously on different tables. In psychoanalysis, the concept of at-one-ment/unison, which Bion introduces to signify the event of the happy emotional encounter between mother and child or patient and analyst from which "order" (structure, psyche) is generated, means nothing more than this.

It is significant that the conflict between Antigone and Creon revolves around a funeral.[64] The process of transfiguring the most natural, material, and absolute thing we know, death, into spirit or soul—which can only happen if people agree to perform certain actions, namely burial—in itself denies the metaphysical, unmediated value that Antigone instead gives to the ritual. But the fact is that a divine thing can only happen as an event if it becomes a human affair, performed by human beings. If he were buried,

Polynices would be recognized as a member of the community even after his death, and not just as the corpse of an animal. At the same time, in terms of the claims of the "Enlightenment" (the seductions of the *Aufklärung*, so to speak, to which Creon is susceptible), the return to the earth is a powerful reminder of the ground[65] from which all our determinations emerge, but which remains inaccessible to the intellect.

The burial is also an allegory of the process of the dialectic of subjectivation, of elevation by removal, what Freud would call sublimation by repression. As Brandom[66] writes, "The *polis* and the family *are* both recognizable communities. Sittlich *substance* (Spirit) *is is* synthetized by reciprocal recognition. Making explicit the commitments that are implicit in *sittlich* practices requires giving up the practical understanding of *Sittlichkeit* as immediate".

Finally, at a more "molecular" level, burial is the negation to which the ego is subjected every time it encounters the other in order to be born, thus allowing it to be born with itself. In this respect, the passage from the *Phenomenology* in which Hegel[67] explains the "contagious" quality of the Ego is extraordinarily illuminating:

It is the force of speech as that which accomplishes what is to be accomplished, for language is the *existence* of the pure self as the self. In language, the *singular individuality* of self-consciousness *existing for itself* comes into existence so that it is *for others*. Otherwise, the *I* as this *pure* I *is* not *there*. In every other expression, the I is submerged in an actuality, in a shape from which it can from out of its action as well as from out of its physiognomic expression, and it leaves behind an incomplete existence, a soulless existence, in which there is always too much as well as too little. However, language contains the I in its purity; it alone expresses the *I* itself. This, its *existence*, is, as *existence*, an objectivity which has its true nature in language. The *I* is *this* I – but is just as much *universal*. Its appearance is just as much the self-relinquishing and the disappearance of *this* I, and, as a result, its remaining in its universality. The *I* that expresses itself is *brought to a hearing*; it is an infection[68] in which it has immediately made its transition into a unity with those for which it is there, and it is a universal self-consciousness. – In its being *brought to a hearing*, its *existence* has itself immediately *become fainter*. This, its otherness, is taken back into itself, and its existence is just this: as a self-conscious *now*, as it is there, it is not there, and through this disappearance, it is there. This disappearing itself is thus immediately its lasting. It is its own knowing of itself, and it is its knowing of itself as a self which has passed over into another self, which itself has been brought to a hearing and is universal.

To think thoughts (to dialogue with others in one's mind), to be aware of existing (through language, which "alone" expresses the I itself) and of the existence of others, to communicate with them: all this happens thanks to language. Without language, there would be neither *I* nor the *other*. In its very making (enunciation), language as spirit generates itself and generates the world. It comes out of the "incomplete" and "soulless existence" of the animal state and of the total and unconscious immersion in reality. This process of self-creation, however, implies an affirmation that passes through its very negation ("*become fainter*", "it is not there", "disappearance").

When I say a word (or rather when I just think it), I do not control the totality of its possible meanings and effects. What I intend to say in it and through it "dies" immediately. Unless someone else picks it up and acknowledges it, an act that represents the moment of "unity" or universalization (in psychoanalysis: unison, empathy, emotional attunement), the moment when something that is only mine or only yours becomes ours (universal). In turn, what the other recognizes, after it has been expressed (after it has taken on a 'form'), dies in order to be reborn the moment it is received in me. Something is born out of something else that dies. But this death is not a return to a pre-human state, as it would be for Polynices if he were not buried according to the rites of the law of the family. Instead, what dies is "received", accepted after being denied, transformed into an intersubjective doing of language that actually happens simultaneously according to the surprising figure of the "infection". What we have called self-generation is actually a radically social, collective, communitarian fact.

I have highlighted this passage from the *Phenomenology* in order to show the *work* that the Sophoclean tragedy of Antigone accomplishes as an allegory of the birth of the ego or the process of symbolization. Conversely, we see how this same process finds an insurmountable limit in the various manifestations of splitting to which we give the name of *hýbris* or "arrogance". Arrogance is *against* life. "Burial", on the other hand, amounts to the process by which something dies in order to transfigure itself and live into something else. The physical body dies but remains as a soul, the body of the word dies but remains as meaning and significance. From this point of view, Antigone's final sacrifice is not only the realization of a defeat, but also the recognition that she must die, that is, give up her "absolute" point of view as independent of human determinations. The price of Polynices' burial seems to be Antigone's physical death and Creon's spiritual death, that is, the abandonment of their respective absolute points of view. This is the only way to celebrate the reconciliation between the human and the divine (not between the actors of the drama, but in the audience that witnesses it), that is, between two forms of ethics that are both human, even if they belong to different registers of being.

Again, in all these deaths what Hegel depicts is the work of the negative. And the work of the negative is not "negative"[69] but is at the origin of dialectics and life. One would not understand why, even if we witness a tragic ending, we come out happier from watching a good play in the theatre. In fact, the tragic dimension is only a semblance. What we see every time is the celebration of the work of the negative as the activity that gives aesthetic form and therefore existence. Within us, reconciliation is not unfinished but effective.

1.6 Übermut

In the *Phenomenology*, the word *Übermut* (arrogance) occurs only twice in a paragraph in the same section where Hegel deals with Antigone. Let us use it here to look at our subject from another angle. It is again the theme of mutual recognition introduced by the myth of the struggle between master and servant and already taken up in Sophocles' tragedy. This time the allegory is the arrogance of the rich man who keeps the poor man down. Another literary reference: *Rameau's Nephew* by Jacques Diderot,[70] published posthumously in Leipzig in 1805. The translation was by Goethe, who had received the manuscript from Schiller after various vicissitudes. Hegel came across it, albeit in a different translation, while writing the *Phenomenology* and immediately used it for his own purposes.

It is significant that the novel has a dialogic form. Such a structure itself invokes the dialectical logic of recognition. *Rameau's Nephew* is also a novel that belongs to the tradition of clandestine and subversive literature, and thus, as we shall see, echoes the emotional position of the protagonist. The year is 1761. We are in Paris. In the Café de la Régence, the narrator-philosopher *(Me)* and Rameau *(Him)* meet to discuss various issues: music, humanity, money, genius, lies, dignity. Meanwhile, in the course of

,he conversation, Rameau reveals himself to be a mixture of cynicism and sensitivity, rebellion and buffoonery, imposture, and intelligence.

The grandson of the famous musician (whose first name is Jean-Philippe), he is not as talented. He is fundamentally a failure. To live, he must be content to serve and flatter rich benefactors, of whose human inconsistency he is all too aware. To please them, he must use what Hegel calls the "language of disintegration".[71] It is the essentially "divided" language of flattery and glittering irony. Rameau merely denounces the contradiction but does not have the strength to resolve it. The beneficiary of the generosity of nobles and wealthy bourgeois, he carries within himself a radical division. On the surface he can't help but show gratitude; inwardly, he is full of resentment ("Then his fury would burn in his eyes, and he'd go back to his meal even more enraged"[72]). Rameau knows that his protectors do not really love him, but out of necessity he accepts to live in abjection.

Acutely aware of his own inner laceration, he found it increasingly difficult for him to endure his condition. "There must be a certain dignity attached to human nature which nothing can extinguish. The most trivial thing will awaken it–something trifling", he comments bitterly.[73] And so it happened. One fine day, at the table, he indulged in a bit of insolence and the rich financier Bertin, owner of the last of the palaces where he had made himself at home, threw him out.

Rameau's misfortune was to have chosen the wrong day for his rebellion. Among the guests was not just anyone, but the abbot. At another time, Bertin himself would have admired his wit. This time, in the face of someone who represents the system of norms on which society is based, he is clearly not in the mood for taking risks. In an ironic twist, however, the abbot takes great pleasure in Rameau's joke. The one who doesn't laugh is the patron: "he was blacker and grimmer than Homer's Apollo when he fired his arrows down on the Greek army".[74] Rameau as Agamemnon, in short. Forgiveness does not come. By introducing the figure of the religious into the scene, Diderot draws the reader's attention with extreme precision to the role played by the hypertrophy of the moral conscience (for Freud, the psychic instance of the superego) in preventing Bertin and Rameau from recognizing each other as persons.[75]

Like Agamemnon, who cannot believe that Achilles would even dare to refuse his lavish gifts in exchange for Briseis, even Bertin cannot understand why his jester would renounce his own generosity. But what is really at stake is each man's sense of himself and his own worth. Not only Rameau but also Bertin discovers that he has a false sense of self. He too is the bearer of a split. As a "person" he thinks he is valuable because of his generosity, but since this is not recognized at all, he must realize that he has been self-deceived. In fact, the only thing on which his identity is based, in terms of the value he thinks he has for others, is material wealth. Like an unhappy child, he discovers that no one loves him.

This knowledge is too painful and Bertin removes it. The realization of the "degradation" in which he lives, his own and others' "laceration", is too much for him. It would have the effect of destroying his vision of himself and his place in society. At this point, Hegel[76] continues, "Wealth. [...] stands immediately before this most inward abyss, before this bottomless depth, in which all foothold and substance have vanished, and in these depths it sees nothing but a common thing, a play of its vagaries, an accident of its arbitrary choices. Its spirit is just essenceless opinion, a superficiality forsaken by spirit".

As the game breaks up, Bertin feels the ground beneath his feet crumble, his sense of importance undermined, and he begins to resist arrogance. Hegel[77] comments: "Wealth thus shares this abjectness with its client, but for wealth, arrogance [*Übermut*] takes the place of indignation". The comment is glowing: arrogance is the ointment for the wound of abjection as an extreme state of mortification of the self.[78] The dynamic of arrogance as a response to non-recognition is crystal clear here. It is also a form of "more latent hostility",[79] of resentful demand, that is, a form of revolt against the revolt of the servant, in which the master becomes the servant of his servant.

Arrogance, then, lies in the presumption of possessing the "intimate essence" (the interiority) of another person, and in being completely blind to the anger that welcomes the "generous" offer instead: "In its arrogance [writes Hegel[80]], which fancies that with a meal it [wealth] has earned an alien I-self and as a result earned the subjection of that other's inmost essence, it overlooks the inner indignation of the other self". Bertin is totally lacking in empathy, "It overlooks the fact that all shackles have been completely cast aside; it overlooks this pure disruption, in which, while, to itself, the *self-equality* of being- for-itself has become utterly unequal, all equality, all stable existence has itself been disrupted; this utter disruption itself does the most to disrupt the opinions and point of view of the beneficent actor".[81]

From a psychoanalytic perspective, the degree of contact with this form of falsehood or division is variable for both. It is easy to think that the more money is unconsciously experienced as indispensable for the illusory acquisition of the desired recognition, the more its accumulation becomes the goal to be pursued at all costs—but if we were to substitute "money" for the will or the accumulation of knowledge, the same defense mechanism would obviously be at work.

To sum up, Rameau and Bertin represent two different forms of reified consciousness. Rameau rebels against his parasitic and alienated condition, which he knew but did not imagine would reach this point, and loses his privileges. In this way, he symmetrically unmasks Bertin's false consciousness. Both find themselves dramatically alone in the face of their poverty as human beings,[82] if we admit that to exist is not to exist in oneself, if that were ever possible, but to be "existed" by the other. The act of rebellion triggers a painful awakening in both. The rich man discovers that he was deluding himself when he thought he had the servant's affection and gratitude; the servant has confirmation that the rich man treated him only as a thing, a tool to satisfy his own desires and that his intelligence is ultimately of little use to him. Disillusionment also forces them to realize that there is nothing that can replace the equal relationship of unselfish love and that they need it in order not to live in the alienation of desperate loneliness.

We understand that the positive moment of recognition, when it occurs, can only follow the negative moment. It is a sign that no formal recognition can be effective. Now that Bertin and Rameau are aware of their mutual interdependence, but on a level that is no longer material, they will for the first time be able to recover from the shock and recognize each other as equals.

One final remark. Since Rameau is by definition a "hungry man" and Bertin a "satiated man", it is obvious that the same line of fracture that separates them on the intersubjective level can also appear between the corporeality and the intellect of the same individual. In comparison with the intellect, corporeality seems to occupy a less elevated and less "necessary" position, but in fact they are in a bond of mutual necessity.

Notes

1 Cf. O. Pianigiani, *Vocabolario etimologico della lingua italiana* (Roma: Società editrice Dante Alighieri di Albrighi & Segati, 1907), https://www.etimo.it/?cmd=id&id=1349&md=05f7d7769ec11bb9dd3eccd88f3c1728.

2 Aristotle, *On Rhetoric: A Theory of Civil Discourse*, transl. G.A. Kennedy (Oxford: Oxford University Press, 2007), 117.

3 D. Alighieri, *The Divine Comedy of Dante Alighieri*, transl. H.W. Longfellow (London: George Routledge and Sons, 1867, Boston: Houghton, Mifﬂlin and Company, 1867), 304, https://archive.org/details/divinecomedyofda00dantiala/page/304/mode/2up.

4 W. Whitman, *Leaves of Grass* (New York: J. S. Redfield, 1871), 54. https://archive.org/details/leavesofgrawhit/page/n61/mode/2up?q=kosmos&view=theater.

5 It would be impossible to see arrogance outside of what the psychoanalytic concept of narcissism implies at the level of character description. However, the reciprocal does not apply, because narcissism can take different forms, and it is not necessarily the case that a narcissistic person is also arrogant. Also unlike narcissism, arrogance is not a metapsychological concept.

6 G. Roberti, *Opere. Tomo IV* (Venezia: Tipogr. di Giuseppe Antonelli, 1830), 129.

7 A. da Ferrara (Antonio Beccari), *Le rime* (Patron, Granarolo dell'Emilia, 1972), 72.

8 N. Tommaseo and B. Bellini, *Dizionario della lingua italiana* (vol. I, Turin: L'unione tipografica editrice, 1861), 623.

9 Ibid., 622.

10 Ibid., 623.

11 F. Nietzsche, *Human All-Too-Human: A Book for Free Spirits*, Part I [1878], transl. H. Zimmern (Edinburgh & London: T. N. Foulis, 1919), 290, https://archive.org/details/HumanAllTooHumanPartIFriedrichNietzsche/page/n299/mode/2up?q=arrogance+&view=theater.

12 Cf. S. Freud, "Civilization and Its Discontents," *The Standard Edition of the Complete Psychological Works of Sigmund Freud* 21 (1930): 57–146, 135: "Anxiety is always present somewhere or other behind every symptom".

13 M. Proust, *Remembrance of Things Past*, transl. C.K. Scott Moncrieff (vol. 2, New York: Random House), 955.

14 M. Proust, *Remembrance of Things Past*, 5.

15 S. Freud, "The Interpretation of Dreams," *The Standard Edition of the Complete Psychological Works of Sigmund Freud* 4 (1900): 457: "My experiences of travelling have taught me that conduct of this ruthless and overbearing kind is a characteristic of people who are travelling on a free or half-price ticket."

16 Cf. V. Magrelli, *Vedersi vedersi. Modelli e circuiti visivi nell'opera di Paul Valery* (Torino: Einaudi, 2002).

17 Cf. D.W. Winnicott, *Playing and Reality* [1971] (London: Routledge, 2005), 188: "What does the baby see when he or she looks at the mother's face? I am suggesting that, ordinarily, what the baby sees is himself or herself. In other words the mother is looking at the baby and *what she looks is related to what she sees there*".

18 Cf. S. Freud, "Mourning and Melancholia," *The Standard Edition of the Complete Psychological Works of Sigmund Freud* 14 (1917):237–58, 249: "Thus the shadow of the object fell upon the ego, and the latter could henceforth be

judged by a special[1] agency, as though it were an object, the forsaken object."
See also S. Freud, *Group Psychology and the Analysis of the Ego* (1921). 109:
"these melancholias also show us something else, which may be of importance
for our later discussions. They show us the ego divided, fallen apart into two
pieces, one of which rages against the second. This second piece is the one
which has been altered by introjection and which contains the lost object".

19 On a broadly 'relational' interpretation of sadomasochism, cf. also R. Mancini, *Le logiche del male. Teoria critica e rinascita della società*, 45, italics
added: "The concept of repetition can be found elsewhere in the context of the
Western philosophical tradition, for example in authors such as Kierkegaard
and Heidegger. For both of them, even with their differences, repetition is by
no means something monotonous and taken for granted; rather, *repetition has
to do with freedom in time, it is the repetition of a situation that challenges
freedom*. Indeed, with repetition comes the possibility of taking up in a new
way something essential that has passed but has not been annulled. On the
contrary, in Freud's perspective repetition is predetermined, inherent in the
invariant structure of the drive, which necessarily tends to the restoration of
the original state of an organism." In "Beyond the Pleasure Principle," *The
Standard Edition of the Complete Psychological Works of Sigmund Freud* 18
(1920):1–64, one of the key texts for the theorization of the death drive, Freud
introduces a similar notion of repetition as a symbolizing activity through the
example of his grandson Ernst's spool game. On this, cf. J. Derrida, *The Post
Card: From Socrates to Freud and Beyond* [1980], transl. A. Bass (Chicago:
University of Chicago Press, 1987). Finally, cf. G. Civitarese, "Masochism
and Its Rhythm," *Journal of the American Psychoanalytic Association* 64
(2016): 885–916.

20 W. Shakespeare, *Henry V*, ACT 1, SC. 2, 252–69, Folger Shakespeare Library,
https://shakespeare.folger.edu/downloads/pdf/henry-v_PDF_FolgerShakespeare.
pdf.

21 Ibid., ACT 1. SC. 2, 242–3.

22 Ibid., ACT 1, SC. 2, 293–307.

23 Ibid., ACT 2, SC. 4, 129–35.

24 Cf. S.C. Woodhouse, *English-Greek Dictionary. A Vocabulary of the Actic
Language* (London: Routledge, 1910), 672, https://archive.org/stream/
englishgreekdict027453mbp#page/n681/mode/2up/search/rape; see also, H.G.
Liddel and R. Scott, *A Greek-English Lexicon* (Oxford: Clarendon Press, 1996),
1841.

25 Cf. S. Freud, *Civilization and its Discontents* (1930), 91: "the dwelling-house
was a substitute for the mother's womb, the first lodging, for which in all likelihood man still longs, and in which he was safe and felt at ease."

26 *The Iliad of Homer,* transl. J. H. Dart, 13, no. 1 (1865): 13, v. 344, https://
archive.org/details/iliadhomerineng00dartgoog/page/12/mode/2up

27 Ibid., 8, v. 198.

28 Ibid., vv. 200–4.

29 Ibid., 9, vv. 223–6.

30 Ibid., 10, vv. 240–4.

31 Ibid., 14, vv. 381–3.

32 Euripides, "Iphigenia in Aulis," in *Nineteen Tragedies and Fragments of Euripides*, vol. II, p. 65–155, transl. M. Wodhull, (London: J. Walker, T. Payne, Vernor, Hood & Sharpe & others, 1809), 113, https://archive.org/details/nineteentragedi00wodhgoog/page/112/mode/2up.

33 Ibid., 85.

34 *The Iliad of Homer*, 426, vv. 85–90.

35 Ibid., 196, vv. 372–6.

36 R. Calasso, *The Marriage of Cadmus and Harmony* [1988] (New York: Vintage Books, 1993), 118.

37 Cf. G. Civitarese, "'Caesura' as Bion's Discourse on Method," *International Journal of Psychoanalysis* 89 (2008): 1123–43.

38 G.W.F. Hegel, *The Phenomenology of Spirit*, transl. T. Pinkard (Cambridge: Cambridge University Press, 2018).

39 S. Freud, "Constructions in Analysis," *The Standard Edition of the Complete Psychological Works of Sigmund Freud* 23 (1937): 255–70, 266.

40 On this concept, cf. cf. M.O. Hardimon, *Hegel's Social Philosophy: The Project of Reconciliation* (Cambridge: Cambridge University press).

41 G.W.F. Hegel, *Aesthetics: Lectures on Fine Art, Volume II*, [1835], Transl. T. M. Knox (Oxford: Clarendon Press, 1975), 1218.

42 Ibid., 1217.

43 Sophocles, *The Antigone of Sophocles*, transl. J.J. Chapman (Boston and New York: Houghton Mifflin Company, 1930), 23–4, https://archive.org/details/antigoneofsophoc00soph_0/page/22/mode/2up.

44 Cf. L. van den Berge, "Sophocles' Antigone and the Promise of Ethical Life: Tragic Ambiguity and the Pathologies of Reason," *Law and Humanities*, 215: "Whereas Creon represents the Olympian 'Tagesgötter', Antigone is connected to the 'chthonic Gods' who have their dwellings in the dark earth. To say that one of those parties is 'more right' or 'more divine' than the other is a mistake; neither can claim to prevail above the other. Hegel's analysis of Creon's perspective on law and justice as one-sidedly depending on human reason but equally 'divine' as Antigone's stance on those matters finds solid ground in both the play itself and in Greek thought about law and religion in general. The Chorus repeatedly invokes Zeus as the supreme god who sustains a civilized order, abhorring any rebellious behaviour that may threaten such order from the inside".

45 Cf. G. Civitarese, "Intersubjectivity Ant the Analytic Field," *Journal of the American Psychoanalytic Association* 69, no. 5 (2021): 853–94.

46 D.N. Stern, L.W. Sander, J. Nahum, A.M. Harrison, K. Lyons-Ruth, A.C. Morgan, N. Bruschweilerstern, and E. Z. Tronick, "Non-Interpretive Mechanisms in Psychoanalytic Therapy: The 'Something More' Than Interpretation," *International Journal of Psycho-Analysis* 79 (1998): 903–21, 909.

47 Cf. F. Falappa, *Il cuore della ragione. Dialettiche dell'amore e del perdono in Hegel* (Assisi: Cittadella Editrice, 2006).

48 Cf. M. Heidegger, *Contributions to Philosophy (of the Event)* [1989], transl. R. Rojcewicz and D. Vallega-Neu (Bloomington, IN: Indiana University press, 2012), 19: "Disposition is the diffusion of the trembling of beiyng as event in Dasein". In essence, it is as if what Hegel calls the *Geist* or spirit (the self-conscious life) is run through by continuous shocks that are transmitted to individuals, where they are registered first and foremost as emotions. On this, cf. C. Pasqualin, "Per una fenomenologia dello stupore. Heidegger e l'origine emotiva del pensare", in *La passione del pensare: in dialogo con Umberto Curi,* eds. B. Giacomini, F. Grigenti, and L. Sanò, 547–66 (Udine-Milano: Mimesis, 2011), 558: "The impact (*Stoß*) by which Being is transmitted to man is therefore first and foremost 'pathetic' in nature. Before any of our words, our thinking, acting or creating, Being has already always touched us and therefore enraptured us in its essence."

49 G.W.F. Hegel, *Aesthetics: Lectures on Fine Art, Volume II,* [1835], 1214–5.

50 Cf. S. Freud, "The Interpretation of Dreams," *The Standard Edition of the Complete Psychological Works of Sigmund Freud* 4 (1900), ix: "Flectere si nequeo Superos, *Acheronta movebo*".

51 G.W.F. Hegel, *Aesthetics: Lectures on Fine Art, Volume II,* [1835], 1219.

52 Cf. R. Mancini, *La fragilità dello Spirito. Leggere Hegel per comprendere il mondo globale,* 56: "Indeed, it is the relation as such that causes him deep distrust, if 'relation' means interaction or encounter between subjects that are different and truly autonomous. Hegel's basic attitude leads him to accept and dialectically develop relation only when it is a movement within the same identity".

53 Sophocles, The *Antigone of Sophocles,* 12.

54 On this point, cf. J. Lacan, *The Ethics of Psychoanalysis 1959–1960* [1986], transl. D. Porter(New York: W.W. Norton & Company, 1997), 279, my Italics: "Because he is abandoned to the dogs and the birds and will end his appearance on earth in impurity, with his scattered limbs an offense to heaven and earth, it can be seen that Antigone's position represents the radical limit that affirms the unique value of his being without reference to any content, to whatever good or evil Polynices may have done, or to whatever he may be subjected to. ... *The unique value involved is essentially that of language.* Outside of language it is inconceivable, and the being of him who has lived cannot be detached from all he bears with him in the nature of good and evil, of destiny, of consequences for others, or of feelings for himself. That purity, that separation of being from the characteristics of the historical drama he has lived through, is precisely the limit or the *ex nihilo* to which Antigone is attached. It is nothing more than *the break that the very presence of language inaugurates in the life of man*".

55 Cf. J. Stewart, *The Unity of Hegel's "Phenomenology of Spirit": A Systematic Interpretation* (Evanston, Illinois : Northwestern University Press, 2000), 300, italics added: "The human law, or what Hegel calls 'the law of universality', is ethical substance that is *conscious* of itself [...] The divine law, on the other hand, is ethical substance that is manifested in immediate action. This law is unknown and *unconscious*".

56 Cf. M. Heidegger's concept of 'equiprimordiality' in M.A. Wrathall, ed. *The Cambridge Heidegger Lexicon* (Cambridge: Cambridge University Press, 2021).

57 Cf. R. Mancini, *La fragilità dello Spirito. Leggere Hegel per comprendere il mondo globale*, cited.

58 G.W.F. Hegel, *The Phenomenology of Spirit*, 274–5.

59 S. Freud, "Civilization and Its Discontents", *The Standard Edition of the Complete Psychological Works of Sigmund Freud* 21 (1930): 57–146, 126.

60 D.W. Winnicott, *Playing and Reality* [1971] (London: Routledge, 2005), 189.

61 Cf. F. Nietzsche, 1887, *On the Genealogy of Morals* (New York: Vintage Books, 1967), 119: "There is *only* a perspective seeing, only a perspective 'knowing': and the *more* affects we allow to speak about one thing, the *more* eyes, different eyes, we can use to observe one thing, the more complete will our 'concept' of this thing, our objectivity,' be."

62 Cf. S. Freud, "Five Lectures on Psycho-analysis", *The Standard Edition of the Complete Psychological Works of Sigmund Freud* 11 (1910): 1–56: "The arrogance [*Dünkel*] of consciousness (in rejecting dreams with such contempt, for instance) is one of the most powerful of the devices with which we are provided as a universal protection against the incursion of unconscious complexes. That is why it is so hard to convince people of the reality of the unconscious and to teach them to recognize some- thing new which is in contradiction to their conscious knowledge."

63 G.W.F. Hegel, *The Phenomenology of Spirit*, 67.

64 On Section A of Part VI of the *Phenomenology*, where Hegel talks about Antigone, and the significance of burial as a recognizing practice, cf. R.B. Brandom, *The Spirit of Trust. A Reading of Hegel's Phenomenology* (Cambridge, MA: The Beknap Press of Harvard University Press, 2019), 481: "The significance of burial is to turn something that otherwise merely *happens* into something *done*".

65 Cf. L. Braver, *Groundless Ground. A Study of Wittgenstein and Heidegger* (Cambridge, MA: MIT Press, 2012).

66 R.B. Brandom, *The Spirit of Trust. A Reading of Hegel's Phenomenology* (Cambridge, MA: The Belknap Press of Harvard University Press, 2019), 486.

67 Hegel, *The Phenomenology of Spirit*, 294–5.

68 In this passage, Hegel indicates the (positive) bonding function of 'contagion' [*Ansteckung*], as it leads to self-consciousness. In re-taking Le Bon and McDougall's theses, Freud (*Group Psychology and the Analysis of the Ego*) instead uses the term "contagion [*Gefühlsansteckung*]" mostly to refer to the negative qualities of the crowd, to the "exaltation or intensification of emotion produced in every member of it" which he describes as an "automatic compulsion [...] to remain in harmony with the many" (84) or increased arousal by mutual induction. The individual fused into the mass, Freud writes, may find safer to "hunt with the pack [but the German expression is 'mit den Wölfen heult': literally, 'howling with wolves]" (85) - hence his Hobbesian view of humanity and the unconscious, here equated with the crowd.

69 In psychoanalysis, the concept that we can make 'correspond' to the Hegelian dialectic of recognition is Melanie Klein's concept of projective identification.

70 D. Diderot, *Rameau's Nephew*, transl. I.C. Johnston (A Project Gutenberg of Australia eBook, 2002), https://gutenberg.net.au/ebooks07/0700101h.html.

71 Cf. Hegel, *The Phenomenology of Spirit*, 300: "However, the self here sees its certainty of itself as such a certainty that is the most essenceless, as the pure personality absolutely devoid of personality. The spirit of its gratitude is thus the feeling of how this deepest abjectness is also the deepest indignation. While the pure I itself intuits itself as external to itself and as disrupted, it is in this disruption that everything which has continuity and universality, everything which is called law, good, and right, has come undone and met its downfall. All equality has been dissolved, for what is present is the *purest inequality*."

72 D. Diderot, *Rameau's Nephew*.

73 Ibid.

74 Ibid.

75 On the concept of 'person', cf. R. Esposito, *Persons and Things: From the Body's Point of View* [2014] (Cambridge, UK: Polity Press, 2015).

76 Hegel, *The Phenomenology of Spirit*, 301.

77 Ibid., 301.

78 D. Diderot, *Rameau's Nephew*, cit "Why else do we so often see devout people so hard, so angry, so unsociable? It's because they've imposed on themselves a task which isn't natural to them. They suffer, and when one suffers, one makes others suffer."

79 Cf. S. Freud, "The Future of an Illusion," *The Standard Edition of the Complete Psychological Works of Sigmund Freud* 21 (1927): 1–56, 12: "If, however, a culture has not got beyond a point at which the satisfaction of one portion of its participants depends upon the suppression of another, and perhaps larger, portion—and this is the case in all present-day cultures—it is understandable that the suppressed people should develop an intense hostility toward a culture whose existence they make possible by their work, but in whose wealth they have too small a share. In such conditions an internalization of the cultural prohibitions among the suppressed people is not to be expected. On the contrary, they are not prepared to acknowledge the prohibitions, they are intent on destroying the culture itself, and possibly even on doing away with the postulates on which it is based. The hostility of these classes to civilization is so obvious that it has caused the more latent hostility of the social strata that are better provided for to be overlooked. It goes without saying that a civilization which leaves so large a number of its participants unsatisfied and drives them into revolt neither has nor deserves the prospect of a lasting existence".

80 G.W.F. Hegel, *The Phenomenology of Spirit*, 301.

81 Ibid., 301.

82 Cf. C. De Bortoli, "Osservazioni sul ruolo del linguaggio nel VI capitolo della *Fenomenologia dello spirit,*" *Post filosofie* 3 (2007): 73–108.

Chapter 2

The Arrogance of Psychoanalysis

2.1 Arrogance, Curiosity, Stupidity

What prompted me to write about arrogance was undoubtedly a certain sense of unease, even dismay, at the signs of degradation that I seem to perceive in civic life. I have outlined them in the introduction and I will return to them briefly at the end of the book, but the idea did not arise, at least not consciously, from current events. It was rather a matter of extending a specific interest to more general considerations. As I have already said, it all began with a commentary[1] on a short text by one of the most important authors in contemporary psychoanalysis, Wilfred R. Bion,[2] which is entitled, in fact, "On Arrogance"—in Italian, "L'arroganza" or "La superbia [*pride*]".[3]

It must be said at once that the latter is an incorrect translation. As we have seen, arrogance, which is often associated with pride, is not pride. The former has a negative connotation, but not the latter, which can also refer to something great, splendid, excellent, etc. Since Bion's essay, in a very original way, questions not only the sick individual but also the institution that has to treat him, it seemed to me that the dynamic he highlighted could be taken as a model for what happens in other institutions and ultimately in society in general. My opinion is that in this essay Bion was essentially writing his version of Freud's *Civilization and its Discontents*.

Therefore, having given a general definition of arrogance, and after having "embodied" it in all its complexity in some characters of fictional literature, I will now summarize and briefly discuss Bion's essay. From the psychology of arrogance in the individual and in the group-institution of psychoanalysis that is supposed to deal with it, in the next chapter I will instead try to extend the discourse to the broader scope of the society and culture in which we live. Again we will be in dialogue with one of the most famous texts of psychoanalysis, *Civilization and its Discontents*, precisely.

DOI: 10.4324/9781032669427-3

In his essay, Bion says that he happened to observe in some severe patients, only apparently neurotic, the sparse recurrence of elements of curiosity, arrogance, and stupidity. Not the words, of course, but what the words denote. In them, this triad of "symptoms" would be the sign of a "psychological disaster". It is as if we were standing in front of the scattered ruins of an ancient civilization, trying to imagine what might have happened. The violence of the disaster was such that it left the mind in a state analogous to that of these ruins. In fact, the patients who suffered from it lost contact with reality and became psychotic.

We immediately realize the extent of what Bion was announcing when he read this paper at the congress of the International Psychoanalytical Association (IPA) held in Paris in 1957.[4] It is as if he said: look, I have discovered a new disease whose characteristics are these and these. In addition to curiosity arrogance and stupidity, the patient exhibits a paradoxical behavior that analysts call "negative therapeutic reaction".[5] It seems that things are going well, but the therapist notices that instead the patient is getting worse instead. This kind of resistance to healing, which Freud attributed to the action of the death instinct, manifests itself in various ways. Patients begin to show a certain disorganization of language, to the point where it is difficult to understand them. Then, they somehow attack the analyst, not so much for the specific contents of his interpretations, but for the function he embodies (and which psychoanalysis embodies) of someone whose job, in turn, is to be curious and to carry out a kind of investigation.[6] Because of these characteristics, the cure really takes on the double meaning that the word φάρμακον implies, that is, both cure ("drug" in the common meaning) and "poison".[7] How can you cure someone of their arrogance curiosity and stupidity if in practice you behave according to the same principles?

To find a solution to this paradox—this is Bion's perspective, but it is also always the perspective of the treatment—is to absorb the virus one wants to eradicate in an amount that does not cause the disease but activates the individual's defenses. In essence, analysis is a dialectical process that rejects a rigidly binary way of thinking. Nothing is excluded or included; if anything, exclusion always involves some degree of inclusion and vice versa. It is the same logic of immunization that is supposed to guard the boundaries of the body: "the immunitary logic, is based more on a non-negation, on the negation of a negation, than on an affirmation".[8] In the same way, different degrees of "alienation", that is, of permeability to what is presented as foreign to the self, can contribute both to the establishment of the ego and to its enslavement. The different fates of psychic immunization are a matter of degree. We intuit that it makes no sense to see the individual as a closed and isolated (monadic) system. Subjectivity and intersubjectivity are to be understood as two sides of the same coin that we call 'subject'.

For Bion, therefore, the problem is no longer just one of certain patients who are sicker than one would think and their accessibility to treatment, but of psychoanalysis itself, which claims to deal with them. A problem of the psychology of the individual reflects a problem of the psychology of the group (in this case the psychoanalytic institution). Indeed, Bion adopts Karl Kraus's[9] caustic aphorism, according to which "psychoanalysis is the mental illness for which it regards itself as therapy" and that the best it can do is to turn its ability to listen to itself in order to cure itself of this absurd claim. The triad of arrogance, curiosity, and stupidity that characterizes a certain class of patients is also a problem for the discipline that is supposed to treat them.

Something is wrong. What should we do? We could take Kraus's paradoxical suggestion seriously. It is not that psychoanalysis has never done so. The history of psychoanalysis could be told in terms of the progressive conquest of its own radical principle of uncertainty, as a series of acquisitions to provide the analyst with new conceptual tools (transference, countertransference, projective identification, enactment, reverie, field, etc.) that allow him to appeal to his own subjectivity, to take into account his own unconscious impulses and desires,[10] to use his own unconscious as a kind of radar to sense how the analytic relationship is developing. Like ultrasound or ultraviolet rays, the "facts" of analysis elude the senses. They are emotions, events that are in themselves invisible, impalpable, and ineffable. They cannot be put into words. Let us also consider that here Bion raises the general problem of whether or not these patients, who were previously considered unsuitable for analysis, can be cured.

To take Kraus at his word, then, in this short and sparkling essay is to start from scratch, to reinterpret what for psychoanalysis, since Freud onwards, has been the principle of principles: the Oedipus theory; and, as we know, Oedipus is a man who understands what *hýbris* is. The diagnosis and "cure" of psychosis in psychoanalysis lends itself by analogy to guessing what the "psychosis" of the society in which we live might be. It is another of the paradoxes of arrogance. As mentioned earlier, the "arrogant" characters in that mirror of life that is literature can be counted on the fingers of one hand, and it is hard to find any of them of rank. This is confusing, given the centrality of Oedipus in Greek tragedy and in psychoanalysis. But it may be because, with Bion, we are misled by the disturbing enormity of patricide and incest. The two "absolute" crimes make us blind to the real crime of Oedipus, from which the rest is born, which is arrogance; and this, despite the fact that we can say that the concept of *hýbris*, that is of arrogance toward the gods, is at the heart of classical Greek culture, and therefore of all our culture. Its centrality in psychoanalysis is evidenced both in the Freudian concept of the oedipal complex, and in the Kleinian concept of the early oedipus; and finally, as we are seeing, in Bion's new interpretation of it.

2.2   Oedipus and the Will to Know

Now, to question the Oedipus of psychoanalysis is a risky move. Indeed, Bion claims that it is only a shift of emphasis. But it is not. When he begins with such a rhetorical assertion, he is saying the opposite. What he is proposing is nothing less than a rejection of Freud's interpretation of Oedipus. It is like breaking a taboo. At the heart of the Oedipal story is not the sexual crime, Bion argues, but Oedipus' stubbornness in wanting to know the truth at any price. No more patricide, no more incest, but the most significant scene is the one in which the tragic hero meets the Sphinx.

Let us quickly grasp the incredible scope of this departure from theory and its reception in popular culture. It is like saying that at the origin of psychic suffering, there are no longer conflicts related to sexuality but to identity. The content is different from Vernant's,[11] but it is as if Bion were anticipating the title of his famous essay "Oedipus without the complex". The conflict remains, but it is transferred to another terrain. Perhaps it is no coincidence that, while depictions of the scene of the patricide or of Oedipus with Jocasta are rare, depictions of Oedipus with the Sphinx are numerous and highly suggestive, from Moreau to Bacon, from Khnopff to Ingres, and so on.

2.2.1   So, What Happens?

The Sphinx is a monster with the face and bust of a woman, the body of a lioness, and the wings of an eagle. Stationed at the gates of Thebes, which is in the grip of the plague, it devours all those who cannot solve the riddle it poses.[12] More astute than his unfortunate predecessors, Oedipus solves it. Defeated, the Sphinx kills herself. Oedipus then triumphantly returns to Thebes, becomes king, and marries Jocasta, with whom he has two sons, Eteocles and Polynices, and two daughters, Antigone and Ismene. This is the beginning of the long story of the Labdacid dynasty, told by Aeschylus in the Oresteia, which paves the way for the suicide of the Sphinx. But even at this point, the question arises as to whether the Sphinx is really dead, or can die, or how the epilogue to this episode of the myth can be read other than literally.

First of all, the Sphinx is a demonic monster, the daughter of Orthrus and Echidna, and therefore of the Chthonian gods. Could she ever die? Could her most spectacular death not be read as a vaticinium, expressed not in words but in gestures and behavior, as if to say that the meaning of existence cannot be expressed in words? Secondly, it is equally inescapable to ask what kind of victory Oedipus achieves. Although he saves the city from the epidemic, he inevitably meets a tragic fate, since another mystery remains unsolved, namely the murder of Laius. The impression is therefore created that "defeating the Sphinx" is a false solution, as it is whenever we substitute abstract intellect for reason; moreover, it is a solution that leads to ruin.

Rivers of ink have been spilled on the interpretation of this scene, but this is not the place to recount it. My aim is to use the filter of Bion's essay to treat the theme of arrogance from a psychoanalytic point of view. From this point of view, the question to be asked is: what can it mean that the crime of Oedipus is not incest, but the claim to solve the riddle of the Sphinx?

I chose the word "claim" deliberately. We must by no means take it for granted, as we did with the death of the Sphinx, that Oedipus will really succeed in finding a solution. It takes little to formulate this doubt. The riddle is a child's riddle; it is too simple. In this apparent ease lies its oxymoronic nature, the obscure vehicle of a terrible truth.[13] There must be something else. Oedipus, himself a living enigma, thinks he has solved it by giving the answer we all know: the animal that walks first on four legs, then on two, and finally on three is man. But can Oedipus say that he really knows who this "man" is? Certainly not. Otherwise, it would not be understandable why he spends the rest of his painful existence trying to find out who he really is. The Sphinx's question should be rephrased as follows: do *you* know who you are? Can *you* say that you really know yourself? Can a man presume to know himself, his heart, his soul?

The question is therefore deceptive and subtly ironic, only apparently simple, and Oedipus' victory is completely illusory. In reality, it is a question that cannot be answered. The only answer that can be given is that the answer is the question itself. As Blanchot[14] writes, and as André Green[15] said he shared with Bion on the occasion of one of their meetings, "The answer is the misfortune of the question". This is a formula that I have sometimes shared with my patients, adding that if you ask questions you only get answers. Myths, as we know, are narratives which, by their very nature, stage the impossibility of ever arriving at an origin, a cause, a principle. It would therefore be futile to reduce their creative ambiguity, which is also that of art in general, to contradictions and thus to "riddles" that can be identified and "solved".

We must therefore accept the idea that the Sphinx, because of what it represents, can die and *not* die (or that it can be continually reborn); that Oedipus saves Thebes but loses himself; that he is guilty but, as Sophocles has him say in *Oedipus at Colonus*, not really guilty; that he cannot avoid responding to the challenge of the Sphinx, knowing that the enterprise is futile, nor can he avoid questioning the oracle about Laius' fate, ignoring Tiresias' contrary opinion. In fact, Oedipus' fate seems to be subject to a kind of invincible compulsion to repeat himself.[16] In the episodes of patricide, of the encounter with the Sphinx, of incest, but even before that in his life in Corinth, in the topical moments in which he seems to be in control of himself, in reality, he is always played by fate (ἀνάγκη). For someone who claimed to have the sharpest vision of others, the result, as we know, is self-blinding and exile, events that in Oedipus at Colonus act as a prelude to the serene acceptance of death.

2.2.2   What Then Is Oedipus' Guilt?

As Bion writes about the patients he's talking about and the psychoanalysis that's supposed to cure them, it's about wanting to know the truth "at any price". Oedipus only becomes himself, a man who embodies humanity while respecting its limits, after he has revealed not the false but the true enigma. At first, he is boundless, arrogant, tainted by *hýbris*, overestimating his own wisdom. Life will teach him that the only knowledge given to him comes from experience and pain; and bitterly, in essence, that it is the knowledge of not knowing.

Now, *hýbris* is the specific word that Sophocles uses for "arrogance". Essentially *hýbris* means "violence" and disregard for the laws. It is therefore opposed to *dike*, i.e., "rule", "custom", or "justice".[17] As the Chorus[18] recites: "'Tis Pride [*hýbris*] that breeds the tyrant; drunken deep/With perilous things is she,/Which bring not peace: up, reeling, steep on steep/She climbs, till lo, the rock-edge, and the leap [not the Sphinx!]/To that which needs must be [*anánke*, i.e. 'fate']".

On the other hand, at the beginning of *Oedipus at Colonus*, as soon as he enters the scene, in addition to age and suffering, among the "masters" that keep him alive Oedipus mentions γεννα̃ον, which means noble origin, royal blood or "nobility of mind", and which is sometimes rendered as "pride". By choosing this term, Sophocles ambiguously but effectively outlines the transformation that takes place in Oedipus as he moves from one drama to another. One single word conveys the idea that he is still proud of his origins but also aware of his *hýbris*.

2.3   A New Syndrome

Having reached this point, we have already learnt some interesting things: like Oedipus, there are patients who have lost contact with reality and who show arrogance, stupidity, and curiosity; and then, more or less between the lines, there is a theory and a technique of treatment which, having absolutized a certain interpretation of Oedipus, deludes itself, like Oedipus, into being able to solve the riddle of its patients' psychosis. In doing so, however, it reveals itself to be "defective" or "psychotic". The common element is the presumption (arrogance) of being able to know the truth "at any cost", the desire to do so—but superficially (curiosity), the illusion of having really grasped it (stupidity). In Lacan's words, the analyst puts himself in the position of the *subject-supposed-to-know*, but not ironically, which means that he does not distance himself from it. The structure of Bion's essay mimics that of *Oedipus Rex*. Just as Oedipus rejoins his criminal self, the analyst gradually discovers himself in the guise of the "obstructive object".

The other striking aspect of the story of Oedipus is that he does nothing but ask (the oracle, his adoptive parents, Tiresias, etc.). By definition, Oedipus is the man who asks, who stops at nothing in order to know. It is this compulsion to always look back that characterizes him much more than the crimes for which he is famous. One aspect that has been noted[19] is that Oedipus puts so much pressure on himself that he is not even really aware of what he is doing. Impulsiveness is therefore also one of his character traits that prevents true knowledge. In short, there is no figure better suited than Oedipus to allegorize the risks of interpretation.

However, since psychoanalysis, unlike philosophy, is not only theoretical but also empirical, (it is the famous Freudian concept of *Junktim*[20]), Bion returns to question clinical experience. What happens to these patients? Apart from what I have already mentioned, the regression that inexplicably follows a series of gradual improvements, the aspect that needs to be further clarified is the attack on the analyst, not for the content he expresses, but for the function he plays. Bion speaks of a double phenomenon. On the one hand, it happens that the patient acknowledges to him, unlike himself, that he is able to endure certain things; on the other hand, he thinks that there is something that the analyst just cannot grasp.

There seems to be a contradiction, but there is not. In fact, there are two different levels. The first level is that of introspection and interpretation expressed in words. The second has more to do with empathy, non-verbal communication, and the ability to absorb the other person's anxiety, to contain it and, as it were, to return it to him after having extracted the excess of persecution. At a certain point, the patient regresses to such an extent that symbolic verbal communication becomes impossible. Obviously, it is on the second level, the level not of dry intellectual knowledge but of affective experience, that the essential game is played. The fact that the patient begins to speak in an incoherent and fragmented way also takes on the meaning of an indirect communication addressed to the therapist, as if he were indicating to him that if they continue in the same register, things can only get worse. In Hegelian terms, the logic of the abstract intellect would eventually overstep the limits that the integrative logic of reason, if it were efficient, would impose on it instead.[21]

I will omit all the detailed steps by which Bion matures his conviction because they are too technical. In essence, he comes to understand that whenever he privileges verbal communication, the patient feels a mutilating attack on his own communication systems, which are mostly affective, semiotic, or non-verbal. Meaning prevails over sense, difference resets identity, intellect crushes affective semiosis,[22] and the psyche leaves the body behind. Instead of integrating, the patient depersonalizes. The same process takes place in the dyad of patient and analyst, or in the unconscious field formed by both. An emotional atmosphere is created that does not favor encounter, mutual recognition, affective attunement, or psychic growth. The result is a 'starvation' of the psyche, an impoverishment of the personality.

At this point it should be easy to make the connection with the reinterpretation of the Oedipus myth proposed by Bion. Faced with the enigma of psychosis, the analyst follows the impulse to understand and objectify. He weaves causal links, looks backward at the facts of reality and history. He is blinded by the light of a supposed science. He makes a translation from the unconscious to the conscious, which in fact is not possible without discrepancies. This is exactly what happens when he uses the theory of Oedipus (or any other theory, for that matter) as a passe-partout for interpretation in the sense of decoding or deciphering.[23]

We now have to deal with another problem. Assuming that this split is at the origin of both the patient's psychosis and that of psychoanalysis, what is its significance in the relationship? What idea can we have of why it is produced?

2.4   Psychogenesis of the Cruel Superego

From the point of view of psychoanalysis, each individual is a group of relationships; the subject 'exists' by being in a relationship. For this reason, it is essential to maintain a good balance between the two poles of the "earth", that is, the indistinct intersubjectivity or erotic-affective sociality, and the "sky", that is, the subjectivity made possible by the abstract or conceptual (linguistic) form of the same sociality. When one term erases the other, the split is born and, with it, psychic suffering. On the one hand, we have forms of antisociality, on the other a conformist adaptation to a completely alienated life. The way in which each person continues to seek his or her own balance depends on history, on all that the relationships experienced in the past have left in the inner world.

We always come back to the same paradox that lies at the heart of self-consciousness and therefore of humanity or being: for Hegel, the *I* that is *we*; for Rimbaud, the *I* that is the *other*; in Bion's words, "In any group there can be seen the man who tries to identify himself wholeheartedly with the basic assumption, or wholeheartedly with the sophisticated outlook".[24] The psychic life of the individual and the group is to find a balance in the constant oscillations (which represent the only way in which a balance can be found) between feeling pursued by "arid intellectualism"[25] and feeling overwhelmed by emotions. Within the group, however, Bion observes that it is easier to cooperate in the basic group mode than in the workgroup mode. The same is true of the group "within" the individual. In short, there is always the idea that the process of subjectivation involves work. This work is not to be understood as the distancing of the individual *from* the group, but as a parallel process of differentiation of the individual *within* the group, that is, of both the individual and the group to which he or she belongs. The "subject" can only be such insofar as the subject is "subjected" to the otherness that gives it life.

When he is in the group in basic assumption, the individual feels more vital ("his capacity for co-operation is emotionally most vital in the basic group"[26]). How can this be explained? By definition, the basic group is made up of strong unconscious emotions, and emotions are the most immediate translation of the body's state of reactivity, energy, and sensitivity. Emotions embody the most immediate, direct, and massive activation of the instinctual defenses, which are in charge of survival, first and foremost physical, are the "civil protection" of the individual. Only in the group does the individual discover that he or she possesses certain capacities. Consequently, according to Bion, we must think that the group is "more than the aggregate of individuals".[27] If these capacities are manifested only through participation in a group, one must also think that the very purpose of the group, its natural tendency, is precisely to function according to basic assumptions.

Entering into a mode of working with basic assumptions has the sense of protecting oneself. It is like the acrobat who, having failed to fly with his partner attached to the bar of the trapeze, falls into the void but is saved by the net. Far from being reduced to a mere dysfunctional phenomenon, the basic assumption takes on the significance of an effective life-saving device. The 'contagion' that Hegel presented positively as a means of achieving self-consciousness takes on the paroxysmal and negative tendency highlighted by Freud. However, we should never lose sight of the fact that it has the sense of a glue that must prevent the vase from falling apart. If anything, once the group has acquired a structure of rationality, the question is whether the two modes are able to work in pairs and thus respond flexibly to stimuli.

To outline the harmonious functioning of the individual and the group, we can use Bion's[28] quotation of the Augustinian concept of the City of God: "a right relation with his fellows can only be achieved by a man who has first regulated his relationship with God. [...] McDougall is concerned to cope with basic assumptions by strengthening the work group's capacity to retain contact with external reality, while St. Augustine is elaborating a technique by which a specialized work group is formed with the specific function of maintaining contact with the basic assumption—in particular with the dependent basic assumption". Read secularly, from a psychological point of view this is like saying that only if the emotional threads that weave the common fabric of the indistinct level of intersubjectivity are thick and strong, will the relations between individuals, that is, the interactions between different subjects, be so.

In other words, the ego depends both on the 'Other' as unconscious and sociality and on the 'other' as a concrete person and necessary channel for the first term. Unable to disregard the other, the subject can only oscillate between the risk of losing the object [29] and the risk of being too close to it; in other words, between two opposite but coinciding forms of "absence". In schizoid personalities, in which psychotic thinking predominates, this oscillation becomes unbalanced. In these personalities, we find a particularly cruel, precocious super-ego which, compared to the needs of the id, ends up preventing the mediating function of the ego. It seems to "deny development and existence itself". As in certain sects (including psychoanalytic ones), the reality principle is not fully developed. Instead of an emotional attitude of openness and hospitality, we find "the exaltation of a 'moral' outlook and a lack of respect for truth. The result is spiritual starvation and stunted growth".[30] As we know, moralism tends to make room for abstract, preconceived ideas and therefore little respect for human interest. It rigidly adheres to the norm at the expense of humanity and vitality. It tends to turn people into robots, making them incapable of 'feeling'.

The aggressive tone toward the other, which easily colors arrogance, is only the external and visible face of the invisible aggression that the subject turns against himself. The unresolved, and perhaps unresolvable, question of its source is played out between two different conceptions of aggression in general, whether primary, innate, or secondary and determined by frustrations imposed by the environment. This is the subject Freud deals with in *Civilization and its Discontents*. It is no small matter. Related to it is the question of whether happiness is possible or whether we are destined to be unhappy. Our ideas about love and civilization also come into play.

We can hypothesize, then, that the early and cruel superego develops in subjects for whom, in the first caring relationship with the object, the experience of no breast or the absence of breast that is at the origin of thought is not tolerable.[31] In other words, in the intermittent rhythm of positive and negative "realizations" given by the encounter of a pre-conception of the breast with the concrete satisfaction, and then by the encounter with a non-satisfaction, the experience of the negative prevails, that is, the painful feeling of absence. The object that provides the truth-as-food-for-the-mind is "moth-eaten". When things are so irreparable as to lead to the structuring of a psychotic personality, the cruelty of the superego merely reflects the degeneration of any experience, however trivial and limited, of the absence of the object into a feeling of terror approaching the experience of the annihilation of the self. The reason is that the slightest absence would be a catastrophe. As Frances Tustin[32] imagines for autistic children, absence is felt as the amputation of a part of the body.

The cruel superego is formed because the fear of losing the object, which is the source of bodily integrity even before the spiritual, urges the subject to please it in every way. The subject lives as a sacrificial victim, always trying to reconcile with a cruel inner god.[33] To preserve itself, the superego gives a very rigid interpretation of the rule dictated by the object (or by the parental couple) and now internalized. The abstract law ignores the living body and no longer interprets its needs. An important part of the population is no longer represented in the parliament of the Ego. The regime is no longer democratic but tyrannical, with a warlike economy and legislation. Needs that are not essential for mere survival are relegated to second place or sacrificed.

At the root of the split is therefore the anguish of suffering a trauma. This is to be conceived along a continuum that goes from signal anxiety to fright. The former is useful because it alerts us and helps us to avoid the trauma, while the latter produces it. If we wanted to schematize, the sequence would be trauma $\rightarrow$ distress $\rightarrow$ split $\rightarrow$ symptom. The likelihood that distress, which when intense is close to fright, will produce trauma, given the same stimuli and the availability of external resources, depends on how the individual's internal world is structured. To use a simple formula, we could say that trauma is a function of unconscious fear ($t=f(F)$). In other words, it is unconscious fear that acts as a multiplier in terms of the impact of a traumatic stimulus, to the point where it is able to overcome the individual's psychic defenses.

It is important to have an idea of how a moral self is born. For example, the neurotic, and even more so the psychotic, is hypermoralistic. He does not allow himself the slightest deviation from the object. Even if, as in the case of *Psycho*,[34] he eliminates it. When this is the imprint received from the primary relationship, the infant's instinctive reaction is to stick to the object in order to plug its holes. The total identification with the ruthless object, the non-distance from it, drastically reduces the degree of freedom of the subject compared to the norm. Responses to stimuli tend to become rigid or almost "automatic". As a minimal differentiation from the object, mere existence is already a guilt. As in Kafka's *Trial*, the dominant feeling is fear and a kind of passive resignation. One understands then that the absolute superego, as well as any form of moralism, is *against* life.

For us, the world is never only the visible world, but also the invisible world, which we unconsciously identify with the object, with the Other. When I fall ill, it is because I have not sacrificed enough for my inner God. It means that God no longer "sees" me. So I have to be harder on myself— which of course leads to anger at the object with which I am identified. Only then can I hope to regain his love and continue to exist. This is the starting point for any form of psychic suffering. If I have a cruel deity inside me, I have to atone. I cannot differentiate myself, i.e. separate myself from the object. To be myself, to try to become what I am, would be to sin, to enter the no-man's-land of guilt. My life disappears in the "law" that I am forced to follow to the letter because I now live in fear.

The cruel superego expresses the imperative to transcend my limitations. In the filigree of this movement of ascent to an ideal ego, we see well in reality that what is at work is an attempt to reconnect with the object. The abstract ideality that drives certain people to be so hard on themselves and to live constantly under the banner of a "having-to-be" is a painful and very concrete search for the other. In the same way, the laceration produced by anxiety in the subject, in society as a social subject, can be expressed in the "having-to-be" of public security or health policy or economic growth at any cost. Arrogance is one of the most tragic faces of "having-to-be". A principle is absolutized, it implements a kind of secession, it imposes itself and abstracts itself from all other principles or needs, it excludes all otherness; but to empty oneself of otherness is to empty oneself of self, to impoverish one's humanity.

To understand what happens when splitting occurs, let us read a passage from Bion's[35] *Learning from Experience*. I will later transpose this insight into an image of Barthes that takes us from the level of individual psychology to that of culture and wider society.

A *split* between material and psychical satisfaction develops. [...] Fear, hate and envy are so feared that steps are taken to destroy awareness of all feelings, although that is indistinguishable from *taking life itself.* If a sense of reality, too great to be swamped by emotions, forces the infant to resume feeding, intolerance of envy and hate in a situation which stimulates love and gratitude leads to a *splitting* that differs from splitting carried out to prevent depression. It differs from splitting impelled by sadistic impulses in that its object and effect is to enable the infant to obtain what later in life would be called material comforts *without acknowledging the existence of a live object on which these benefits depend.* [...] The need for love, understanding and mental development is now deflected, since it cannot be satisfied, into the search for material comforts. Since the desires for material comforts are reinforced *the craving for love remains unsatisfied and turns into overweening and misdirected greed.*

As we can see, the strategy is survival, the tactic is the antithesis of animism. Instead of attributing a living quality to an inanimate object, the point here is to render the living object inanimate, a thing among things. This is the aim of the Freudian death instinct. The result is that you lose contact with your own living substance. If this did not happen, if the subject continued to relate to a "living" object, his envy (i.e., the state of "starvation" from which his hunger for love arises) would grow to the point of becoming destructive. He would no longer be able to control his emotions. He would be consumed by them.

A short clinical fragment. It is the last session before the holidays. A young patient tells the analyst: "There is only one positive side to this separation: that I don't pay". By expressing herself in this way, she feels better because she strengthens the "material" bond that unites them and accepts the pain of disillusionment (the negative side) in relation to the affective bond. She will be able to tolerate the pain thanks to a small physiological split, with a slightly manic flavor. The "positive side" is not that she does not pay, but that, by tying it to the satisfaction of the analyst's concrete needs, she is reassured that the relationship will resume as soon as the period of separation is over.

Splitting works like the insulation around electrical wires, it avoids the short circuit that violent emotions would end up triggering. At the origin of the split, there is always a disturbed relationship with the object, in which envy and hatred could not be mitigated. It is like blocking a contact on *WhatsApp* or deleting it from your agenda.[36] At this point, the other has become indifferent to me. I have removed the tension that arises from difference, that is, from "the emotional complications of awareness of life" and form having "a relationship with live objects".[37] Such a person, Bion continues, is " incapable of gratitude or concern either for himself or others. This state involves destruction of his concern for truth"[38] and the inability to learn from experience. This is only possible if there is an awareness of the emotional experience. If, on the other hand, emotions must be cut away because of their linking function, what remains is only a flawed version of experience, that is, devoid of true meaning. Without emotions, nothing that happens makes sense. In the deepest part of the personality, the "psychotic" part, Bion explains,[39] there is an excessive proliferation of "links which appear to be logical, almost mathematical, but never emotionally reasonable. Consequently, the links surviving are perverse, cruel, and sterile".

As we can guess, material objects can never aspire to satiate such greed, it is not in their power to reflect and recognize the subject so as to make him or her a living person again. The same request for healing addressed to the analyst "takes the form of a search for a lost object and ends in an increased dependence on material comfort; quantity must be the governing consideration, not quality. He feels surrounded by bizarre objects, so that even the material comforts are bad and unable to satisfy his needs".[40]

2.5   The "Psychosis" of Psychoanalysis

In summary, we have seen that the psychoses of the patient, the analyst, and the institution to which he or she belongs correspond to dysfunctional defenses (the ideo-affective *split*) in relation to the distress caused by the traumatic event. The purpose of the defense, to the detriment of the more instinctual part, is to preserve what is most precious to the individual's humanity, namely the ability to represent (intellect, logic, concept), as it is more directly linked to the development of language and self-consciousness. However, if the defense is excessive, it does not lead to psychic growth, but to a state of regression that ends up being self-perpetuating. In the analytic treatment, breaking this vicious circle has to do with something very similar to what Bion advocates in his essay: stripping away the arrogance of the will to know and of abstract knowledge, restoring a line of communication with the "reasons" of the body, putting emotions and affects back at the center of the treatment.

Throughout his life, Bion struggled to renew psychoanalysis by giving it a less ideological, less "religious", or less moralistic basis. It is safe to say that he has worked hard for an ethical psychoanalysis. He did so, however, not as an abstract petition of principle, but by seeking to ground his claim on a solid psychoanalytic understanding. He asked himself what psychoanalysis, with its tools, could say about moralism. Simply put, the equation moralism = moral superiority = cruelty applies to him. Clarifying the basis of moralism is like clarifying the basis of psychological suffering. If there is one axiom that I would feel myself to advance, it is about the universally (hyper-)moralistic origin of psychological suffering. All people who come to the analyst suffer from some degree of dissociation between affectivity and intellect. Abstract reason is usually relied upon to compensate for deficiencies in affective and relational competence. In particular, in these cases the intellect is at the same time too far from the earth and too close to the sky. By "earth" I mean the emotional body, by "heaven" I mean the system of laws that deeply pervades language and thus the rational pole of the subject.

More generally, however, the moralism of analysts sometimes exudes pedagogy, guilt-ridden interpretation, self-indulgence and the hypo-critical and intrinsically violent irony of those who make it clear (sometimes deliberately) that they are reading you "through". But it can also be the display of a certain ruthlessness, misunderstood as anti-sentimentalism and mystified as familiarity with the psychic mechanisms of the unconscious as inferno[41] or the unconscious as prison: translating from the unconscious into the conscious, allying oneself with the "healthy" part of the patient's ego and seeing madness only in the other. Bion writes that taking the title of psychoanalyst is tantamount to being able, thanks to projective identification "(in which he does not believe), to preen himself on freedom from the psychosis from which he looks down upon patients and colleagues".[42]

Talking about "our psychoanalytic parents", Borgogno[43] remembers that "they were often quite 'phobic' relating and the affects, in front of which they not infrequently posed a sort of diktat that later in life I defined 'No-entry'". And he adds: "if we look at the history of psychoanalysis, sibling groups have, more often than not, been more ruthless and ferocious than their progenitors in remorselessly ditching their travelling companions, either from jealousy or envy". They constituted a community in which "you were always under examination, especially if you wanted to get on; where the atmosphere was always laden with Superego and do's and dont's".

Otto Kernberg's[44] famous 1996 article on the thirty ways to destroy the creativity of trainees in psychoanalytic institutions is a milestone in the history of psychoanalysis. In it, a former president of the IPA, the International Association of Analysts founded by Freud in 1910, from the height of his authority as a scholar and politician, lucidly and courageously describes the power structures of the psychoanalytic institution. The text contains a list of the various methods that can be used to extinguish any trace of originality, enthusiasm, or critical passion; to establish instead an emotional climate of paranoid anxiety,[45] as the most appropriate to keep the group of students in line.

The most effective measures include: preventing the contamination of Freud's theories (Jung, Bion, Lacan…) with other theories; forcing people to study and write extensively about Freud; subliminally conveying the idea that any exercise in critical thinking will ultimately only confirm Freud's ideas and those of the leaders of the local institution; artfully arousing disbelief and indignation about "deviant" schools; maintaining strict hierarchical boundaries between teachers and students.

It is also desirable to relegate the expression of critical remarks to Oedipal problems, thus deserving further "analysis"; to discourage premature writing or attendance at academic meetings; to strictly avoid risks of contagion from alien ideas or from dissident members or leaders of other schools; to proceed at most with cautious inoculation, i.e., to allow only limited exposure and just enough to induce a strong immune response; to make life difficult for "dissidents" in examinations.

It is very useful, then, to discourage the study of modern principles of psychoanalytic technique, teaching instead always from Freud's clinical cases; to cultivate in candidates an appropriate sense of insecurity and humility about the quality of their work, so as to inhibit undesirable personal and creative developments; to prevent dangerous contacts with scholars of other disciplines in order to preserve the purity of the psychoanalytic institution and the idealization of psychoanalysis; but above all, to always maintain discretion, secrecy, and uncertainty about the rules governing the process of access to the "higher" status of training analyst.

From the portrait Kernberg paints of it, it is clear that the aim of the psychoanalytic institution is to blindly preserve itself and to be organized in such a way that any flicker of thought and creativity is instantly extinguished. As he concludes, "Always keep in mind: where there is a spark there may develop a fire, particularly when this spark appears in the middle of dead-wood: extinguish it before it is too late!".[46]

You would think that after such a *J'accuse*, harsh but expressed in a calm and ironic way a quarter of a century ago, analysts would have rolled up their sleeves to reform everything that needed reforming. If you thought that, *you* would show that you had no idea of the resilience of bureaucracy, of the incredible capacity of the institution to protect itself from disintegration and devour everything without moving an inch, nor of the proliferation of violent power devices that lurk within it. It is symptomatic in this respect that Kernberg's article, the most sulfurous written on the subject, is only the second of a triad. In fact, it sits in the middle between two others published in 1986 and then in 2012, respectively, "Institutional Problems of Psychoanalytic Education" and "Suicide Prevention for Psychoanalytic Institutes and Societies".[47]

In the first one, Kernberg had already pointed out aspects such as the climate of indoctrination, the lack of critical spirit, intransigence, ritualism and idealization, the 'surveillance' implemented against the students, the aspects of collusion and institutional corruption at various levels, the paranoid deterioration of the social life of the institute, the split between institutional and "family" instances, the lack of transparency in the evaluation processes and in the criteria adopted in them, intellectual servility, the discrepancy between primary and explicit tasks and the structure of the organization that should pursue them, the excess of discretion that in some cases "turns into hypocrisy and dishonest manipulation", the illusion of "perfect morality"[48] on the part of its most authoritative members; more like a theological seminary than an art academy or a university faculty (of course, this description would fit several university departments like a glove), in which a power elite pursues "scientifically" the goal of self-perpetuation. In this way, Kernberg[49] writes, "Psychoanalysis thus becomes a powerful ideological instrument in combating the unfaithful, in using unconscious motivation of others as a social weapon".

The picture that emerges is bleak, even merciless. The author himself goes so far as to question whether or not psychoanalysis as a scientific field as a whole has anything new to say. However, Kernberg would not be wasting his time, if he did not think it worthwhile to preserve and develop all that psychoanalysis has to offer. Indeed, he notes that "the exciting developments at the boundaries of psychoanalytic theories and technique belie such a narrow and pessimistic view".[50] For example, Bion and other writers who have taken up and extended his ideas tell us one simple thing: that we are now able to focus accurately on the ideological factors of psychoanalysis. This means that we can finally get rid of "Respectable, shoddy, worn-out psycho-analytic, mental 'reach-me-down' mental clichés for the dead-from-the-neck-up!".[51]

From a historical perspective, the origins of the analyst's "moralism" can be traced to Freud's naturalistic approach and his conception of the demonic unconscious.[52] These are the elements for which Ricoeur[53] enrolled him, along with Marx and Nietzsche, in the so-called school of suspicion. But then, we might ask, if he was in this select company, and if he was after all the first 'immoralist' of psychoanalysis (in fact, as he recalls in *Dora*, he was accused of writing equivocal stories and of perverting young girls[54]) what is the role of Bion and others like him who criticized Freudian psychoanalysis? Actually, Ricoeur's famous formula should be revised. It reflects well the suspicious attitude of the traditional analyst, ready to seize and stigmatize the signs of perversion of the unconscious seen as a world turned upside down. I don't know if the same can be said of Nietzsche and Marx in their demystification respectively of the false consciousness of Christianity or of the cultural superstructures of class society.

Bion does not say anything about this, but the hypothesis that he wrote "On Arrogance" inspired by the Greek concept of *hýbris* seems plausible. Oedipus is arrogant because he does not accept the limits of his humanity, curious because his excess takes the form of wanting to know what humans are not allowed to know, and stupid because he confuses true knowledge with the abstract use of the faculty of the intellect.[55] In order to "cure" the analyst (himself) of the poison/drug of the triad arrogance-curiosity-stupidity, Bion then proposes to adopt its negative form, or to renounce "memory" as the presumption to connect facts that explain the cause of psychic suffering, "desire" as the will to know, and "understanding" as the abstract and intellectualistic illusion of having succeeded.

2.6   Negative Capability

I do not wish to be trivially misunderstood. It should be clear, I hope, that the ideological arrogance of which I speak in relation to psychoanalysis has nothing to do with the personality traits of any particular analyst. Rather, it is a purely epistemological problem and, as such, must be placed in a historical framework. When I speak of an "ethical re-foundation", I do not mean that psychoanalysis has been deliberately unethical (which would be unfair and absurd) according to different parameters and historical contexts. I mean that, in my opinion, it should distance itself from the "paranoid" ethos of constant suspiciousness; from that being vigilant, cautious, and wary which, to use the term that Rita Felski,[56] refers to a certain kind of critical analysis of literary texts, concretizes a kind of systematic "oppositionality" (*againstness*).

As Bion pointed out, the institution-as-establishment (I repeat, *any* institution), as the guardian of the group's identity, has a fatal tendency to stiffen and corrupt itself. This happens because it fears being destroyed if it accepts the instances of renewal proposed by its most original and creative members, even if they perform a necessary function for the group to remain vital.

Rather, I am referring to the fact that, from the point of view of critical theory, we are now better able to identify ideological remnants and power relations. The problem, then, is whether such unjustified remnants remain in the new cultural climate of postmodernity. It would be tantamount, for example, to ignore our new awareness of the ways in which relations of domination over minorities and socially weaker groups have been (and still are) insidiously reasserted—even in the way the author uses feminine and masculine pronouns in a text.

At the same time, since it is linked to our concept of truth, I believe that the ethical re-founding of psychoanalysis must go hand in hand with the development of the theory and technique of treatment. What is needed is a paradigm shift that extends the receptivity to the unconscious in the session to 360 degrees, including that of the analyst, to the point of considering that, at least at the level of unconscious communication, there is not an *I/you* but a we or an impersonal subject. This implies a reformulation of the concepts of the unconscious, dreaming, and therapeutic action. One way of doing this is along the lines suggested by Bion and later developed in post-Bionian psychoanalysis.

Let's take an example. A patient keeps telling me about his absent and violent father. How do I listen to this communication? I could stay on the level of psychotherapy in the strict sense and get an idea of the relationship she has with her father at home. I would stay on the level of historical and material reality. But this is not yet the method of psychoanalysis, which focuses on unconscious psychic reality. If, on the other hand, I listen to the dimension of unconscious communication, I could think of the same "absent and violent father" both as a projection onto me (transference) and as an internal object that lives in the theatre of her mind and where the meaning with which she reads the world is constantly generated (uncon-scious fantasy).

There remains, however, another—indeed the most radical—way of us-ing the concept of the unconscious. I could listen to his narrative as an unconscious communication that is not exclusive to the patient, since it is inevitably influenced by my own participation in the analytic conversation. The narrative is no longer something real and external to the analysis, or in-ternal and limited to the patient's inner world. Instead, it becomes an inter-subjective construction, like that of a small group or third mind, formed in the here and now, and which therefore has a 'we' as its author. The analytic relationship takes on the character of a theatrical performance in which the patient and analyst are director, actor, and spectator and whose meaning, with reference to Melanie Klein's theories of play or Judith Butler's[57] per-formative identity, is to construct themselves as subjects.

The consequences of this last possibility are remarkable. When I listen in this way, I make the caesura (split) between material reality and psy-chic reality and the caesura (split) I/you transitive. I rediscover the fund of indistinct intersubjectivity that unites me with the patient, I reset for a moment the differences that separate us, I meet him on a level of equality, outside any relationship of domination. It is the situation of being one that makes the spirit of both grow. I stop being suspicious, I get out of the logic of *who does what to whom*, and I see the story as almost containing a kind of truth, albeit expressed in a dreamlike or allegorical form, about our own emotional functioning.

I think there is no more effective way of conceptualizing what the thera-peutic action of psychoanalysis consists of. At the cost of some simplifica-tion, we can say that we have moved from using the idea of the therapeutic relationship to give experiential grounding to the interpretive translation from unconscious to conscious, to using our theories to enable an authentic experience of mutual recognition. In other words, we rely less on the logic of the intellect and more on the logic of love (*Liebe*).

When it happens, this reconciliation comes not only from what is my personal equation, but also from the skills I have as an analyst. These are expressed, among other things, in a certain way in the use of the concept of the unconscious and of intersubjectivity. Recognition of the other does not take place through a presumption of goodness—mostly just a form of false consciousness—but through the assumption of responsibility, even pain-ful responsibility, for the otherness that inhabits me (what Freud calls the uncanny), for the other in me and me in the other, for one to 'exist' the other and vice versa.[58] This is the moment when authentic recognition is triggered, when the relationship is based on the "logic of love",[59] and no longer on the instrumental logic of knowledge for its own sake or of domination (which are, from a certain point of view, the same thing). It is not only the reconciliation of the *I* and the *You* in the *We*, but also of the body and the psyche in the somato-psychic unity of the subject. If the analyst rediscovers himself each time as one of the protagonists of the *fabula*, thanks to the resetting of the distance and the greater involvement, he cannot but react with more intense emotions and sensations. Even situations that could be stagnant or deadly are immediately revitalized. The psyche returns to the body and the body returns to the psyche.

I think that psychoanalysis, after the many achievements of critical theory, feminism, deconstruction, etc., to which it has contributed so much, needs to regenerate itself. What do I mean by that? That it is a discipline that has strong emancipatory aspects, but also alienating ones. Even if he does not intend to, when the analyst pretends to reveal the unconscious to the patient, that is, when he explains that he systematically misunderstands[60] him because of his infantile neurosis, he ends up, as Bion says, looking down on the patient. In my opinion, if he does this, it is because he does not sufficiently consider his own subjectivity and the role that the unconscious life plays in it. In the folds of the discourse he subtly becomes ideological, judgmental, or pedagogical-moralistic.[61] These poisonous elements stem from Freud's naturalistic approach to the study of the psyche, factors that are understandable on a historical level but, I repeat, in my opinion no longer justifiable today.[62]

A different case, it seems to me, is that of the analyst who considers himself to be completely immersed in the virtual-oneiric climate of the session, who does not want to attribute to himself or to the other the responsibility for the "facts" of the analysis, i.e., to use the perspective of the relationship between two separate subjects, but focuses on the unconscious dual, group, indistinct, or intersubjective level. Adopting this point of view leads him to abandon the suspicious attitude of classical psychoanalysis,[63] which stems from a metaphysical and anti-historical conception of truth.

On the contrary, in the productions of this kind of "third" mind whose existence we postulate at the symmetrical plane of unconscious communication, he sees the veridical reflection of the emotional experience shared in the present encounter. There are so many 'characters' in the analytical dialogue, so many points of view (but also expressed through sensations, reveries, and actions) that he manages to have on the same fact. *His* becomes the exercise of accepting in his own finite the maximum possible infinity. The intersubjective plot of being expands and with it, in parallel, that of subjectivity. The Ego gets empowered.

The device that carries the greatest weight with respect to the reconciling and subjective capacity of analysis is therefore both theoretical and practical. The analyst listens to the analytic dialogue as if it were the dream dreamt by the couple or the small group of two. The shared and unconscious activity of transforming proto-sensory and proto-emotional elements into images endowed with personal (particular) and impersonal (universal) meaning produces narratives that allegorize their own making. Nothing less than shared and unconscious emotional truth is represented in them. The analyst has no choice but to put his trust in the common effort of the search for this truth, and thus in each of the members of the dyad.

The analytical field generated by unconscious communication corresponds to the intersubjective layer of the subject, to the indistinct and common pole which, in each individual, dialectically interacts with the pole of subjectivity to constitute the whole of the subject (or even of the social subject). Starting from this theoretical postulate, the analyst seeks to recompose the I/you split at its base. In essence, the analyst resets to zero the logic of imposition inherent in cognitive operations carried out *on* the other rather than *with* the other. Indeed, from this 'systemic' point of view, it would make no sense to interpret the one as "doing"[64] something to the other or vice versa. It would always be an unconscious "we". Even if this third mind were to deceive itself, the members of the dyad that give it life would still be on a symmetrical or equal level with each other. It can be seen that this symmetrization of the relationship is the opposite of the separating or disjunctive movement that we have outlined as belonging to arrogance. Absolute difference, that is, arrogant closure in one's own partial truth, gives way to the possibility of authentic recognition. Recognition is "authentic" (Heidegger: *eigentlich*) when it entails both an increase in freedom and the capacity to choose the mode of existence.

This way of understanding the workings of the unconscious implies an uncommon negative capacity, namely the ability to set aside what is already known in order to intuit the unknown, to allow oneself to be involved and to be surprised. The process is governed by a principle of systematic doubt, and tolerance of frustration or uncertainty. This principle expresses a precise theoretical and technical position; it is not in the least based on sentimentality or spontaneity. This is an important point. Hospitality to the other cannot be naïve. In analysis, it is not because it passes through the exercise of a sharp critical theory that fosters a particular receptivity to the unconscious.

Fundamentally, understanding involves struggle and work. In the context of treatment, it means the rigorous use of the concept of the unconscious as intersubjectivity and the psychoanalytic function of personality. Acknowledging the common, i.e., "symmetrical", oneiric (poetic or poem-like) capacity of the mind to enact the emotional truth of the relationship at any moment (to specify its sign) allows, in the second instance, to recover the difference, i.e., an asymmetrical perspective on things. The Freudian principle of oneiric "distortion",[65] which refers to a concept of positive truth, is replaced by the Bionian principle of "transformation", which refers instead to a pragmatic and social concept of truth.

In conclusion, we can say that from the point of view of contemporary psychoanalysis, ethics as a principle of uncertainty and the art of hospitality, but, I repeat for the umpteenth time, embodied in precise tools of theory and technique, is the antidote to the spread of fear, trauma, and consequently to arrogance. The Freudian "neutrality [*Indifferenz*]",[66] that is, the assumption that the analyst can be completely neutral, seems to us today to be outdated. The analyst no longer adopts an abstract principle of neutrality, he does not believe that he can function as a "blank screen". Rather, he sees his emotional and unconscious participation in the therapeutic relationship as inevitable; if anything, he adopts the principle of a "sweet", concave, welcoming skepticism.[67]

2.7 The Neutral

For Roland Barthes, the antonym of arrogance is "neutrality". In the beautiful seminar on the concept of "neutral" held at the Collège de France toward the end of the 1970s, the French scholar formulates a very effective definition of arrogance: "Under the word 'arrogance', I gather all the (linguistic) 'gestures' that work as discourses of intimidation, of subjection, of domination, of assertion, of haughtiness: that claim the authority, the guarantee of a dogmatic truth or of a demand that doesn't think, that doesn't conceive of the other's desire. [...] One is assaulted by the arrogance of discourse everywhere there is faith, certitude, will-to-possess, to dominate".[68] It is clear that a common form of arrogance is that which appeals to the evidence of (alleged) facts, to common sense, to the naturalness of things. But "evidence", Barthes notes, should be "dysarrogantized", making it relative, attenuating it, humanizing it in the end.

Still, be careful: the 'concept' is in a certain sense "arrogant" in itself, because it sets differences to zero; as we know from Nietzsche, quoted here: "Every idea originates through equating the unequal",[69] it is a tyrannical and assimilating force. Should we then say no to the concept, stop using it? That would not be possible. Barthes suggests replacing it with metaphor, that is, with "writing". Compared to the immediacy of the voice—Derrida would say to its logocentric or metaphysical aspirations—the mediated expression of writing functions precisely as a process of putting into latency the effect of the presence of the ego to itself and the presumption that is its sign. Writing shields one from the assertiveness and arrogance of discourse.

It is the analyst's tactic to use the dream of the night and reverie to circumvent the power of the intellect, enslaved by the super-ego, to colonize the body, to discipline it, and usurp its rights. To the urgent invitation to take sides, the analyst responds with the negative ability to wait patiently for something that has not yet been thought. The only rule he follows, pragmatic but not utilitarian, is to renounce not preconceptions but predeterminations. The analyst tends to listen carefully, but without memory, without desire, and without understanding.[70] He neutralizes the arrogance of conscience by adopting a form of 'civil disobedience'. He is attentive to gradations, nuances, and shades. Stops, digressions, delays, stumbles, and hesitations are the lexicon that guides his steps in the endless conversation of analysis.

Significantly, nuance comes from "cloud". Is there anything less stony or "dogmatic", even in its visibility, than the piles of vapor that make up the ephemeral matter of a cloud? It is the detail, the small difference, that arrogance would like to dismiss as insignificant. For example, in relation to the technocratic perversion of society, which serves as an immunization against misery, the restriction of personal freedom, and thus the effects of dehumanization. To embrace the "neutral" is then to escape the "fascism" of binary oppositions, if not to transcend the caesura that orders them, to embrace ambiguity. Obviously, this neutrality is not strategic but tactical. It certainly does not aim to exempt the individual from choosing and assuming his responsibilities.

The exercise of doubt does not arise from suspicion. On the contrary, it is more a willingness to give hospitality to the other. The analyst replaces the *I/you* split with the impersonal, third,[71] neutral subject, and in this way adopts the perspective suggested by Barthes: to quote Schwartz,[72] "With the Neutral (a word he always writes with a capital letter) Barthes aimed at the curious task of achieving a domain outside the opposition and conflict of differences that is required of us to make sense of things. He called it a 'seeking', a 'striving' and a 'desire'—'the desire of the Neutral'—that could only be captured in 'sparkles' and 'shimmers'. This entails: -first: suspension (*epoché*) of orders, laws, summons, arrogance, terrorism, warning, will to take possession. -then, going deeper, the rejection of the pure discourse of opposition. Suspension of narcissism."

The invariant of arrogance would therefore be the dogmatic imprint, the absolutizing of difference. Whoever proclaims a dogma also imposes a choice (but it is not a real choice) without delay. Contrary to what Freud thinks about the repression of instincts and the condemnation of a certain unhappiness as the price of civilization, Barthes denounces the "frenzy" (literally, a state of madness) of a civilization that, like a mother with her child, forces it to eat. In fact, the effective figure of modernity is not anorexic asceticism but bulimia: the "society, "doxa, puts itself in the position of the mother: it is accused of forbidding desires, but I find that mostly it dictates them, imposes them, forces their satisfaction."[73]. Barthes goes so far as to denounce the very absence of ideology as the new barbarism (but *"cold, frozen, 'civilized'"*)[74] of a pure technocracy. There is no need for an "ideosphere", that is, a space that is at the same time inhabitable but excluding, which is organized around a given ideology; it is enough to adapt to the dictates of a perfectly sanitized society so as not to impede its mercantile traffic.[75]

Barthes' brilliant insight helps us to see that Bion's essay is not only about the interpretation of the Oedipus tragedy and the fate of psychoanalysis. Bion makes us understand something more, both of the 'small' everyday tragedy of arrogance, and of that which assumes great proportions when it takes the form of the political action of a leader or a party, or represents the unease of the civilization of diffuse and anonymous power, as Foucault outlines with extraordinary clarity throughout his work.

We would say, then, that in all the cases we have grouped together under the concept of arrogance/*hýbris*, the common problem is the lack of contact with reality (the aspect of "psychosis"). At its origin, an irrepressible fear causes a defensive split between intellect and reason. This manifests itself in a wide range of symptoms, but in the end it always reflects power relations.

Notes

1 G. Civitarese, "The limits of interpretation. A reading of Bion's *On arrogance*," *The International Journal of Psychoanalysis* 102 (2021), 236–257.

2 W. R. Bion, "On Arrogance." *International Journal of Psychoanalysis* 39 (1958): 144–146.

3 W. R. Bion, "La superbia" [1958], in *Analisi degli schizofrenici e metodo psicoanalitico* [1967] (Roma: Armando, 1979), 133–141.

4 Cf. D. Meltzer, *The Kleinian Development-Part III: The Clinical Significance of the Work of Bion* [1978], (London: The Harris Meltzer Trust, 2018), 31: "the reading of the paper 'On arrogance' at the Paris Congress struck many people as a shocking display of the very 'hubris' Bion was describing".

5 Cf. S. Freud, "The Ego and the Id." *The Standard Edition of the Complete Psychological Works of Sigmund Freud* 19 (1923): 1–66, 49: "There are certain people who behave in a quite peculiar fashion during the work of analysis. When one speaks hopefully to them or expresses satisfaction with the progress of the treatment, they show signs of discontent and their condition invariably becomes worse. One begins by regarding this as defiance and as an attempt to prove their superiority to the physician, but later one comes to take a deeper and juster view. One becomes convinced, not only that such people cannot endure any praise or appreciation, but that they react inversely to the progress of the treatment. Every partial solution that ought to result, and in other people does result, in an improvement or a temporary suspension of symptoms produces in them for the time being an exacerbation of their illness; they get worse during the treatment instead of getting better. They exhibit what is known as a 'negative therapeutic reaction'".

6 Cf. C. Ginzburg, "Clues: Roots of an evidential paradigm," in *Clues, myths and the historical method* (1979; Baltimore, MD: John Hopkins UP, 1989), 96–125.

7 Cf. J. Derrida, "Plato's pharmacy" [1968], in *Dissemination*, transl. B. Johnson (Chicago: The University of Chicago Press, 1981), 63–117.

8 Cf. R. Esposito, *Immunitas: The Protection and Negation of Life* [2002], transl. Z. Hanafi (Cambridge, UK: Polity, 2011), 8.

9 K. Kraus, *Half-Truths and One-and-a-Half Truths: Selected Aphorisms*, transl H. Zohn (Montreal: Engendra Press, 1976), 77. On the conflicting relationship between Kraus and psychoanalysis, see S. Freud, M. Graf, and K. Kraus, *Otto giorni a Vienna. Psicoanalisi, arte e letteratura* (Turin: Robin, 2013).

10 Cf. M. Wilson, *The Analyst's Desire: The Ethical Foundation of Clinical Practice* (New York: Bloosmbury, 2020).

11 J.- Vernant e Vidal-Naquet, *Myth and Tragedy in Ancient Greece* [1986], transl. J. Lloyd (New York: Zone Books, 1990).

12 Coming from such a chimera, the real question, which is in fact unsolvable, might be about man's animality, that is, his essence.

13 Cf. N. Gardini, "L'enigma", in *Lacuna. Saggio sul non detto*, (Torino: Einaudi, 2014), 135–144.

14 M. Blanchot, *The Infinite Conversation* [1969], transl. S. Hanson (Minneapolis: University of Minnesota Press, 1993).

15 Cf. A. Green, "The primordial mind and the work of the negative," *International Journal of Psycho-Analysis* 79 (1998): 649–665, 657: "I remember how much Bion was struck when I quoted Maurice Blanchot's sentence: 'La réponse est le malheur de la question.' He used that proposition many times".

16 Cf. S. Freud, "New Introductory Lectures on Psycho-Analysis," *The Standard Edition of the Complete Psychological Works of Sigmund Freud* 22 (1933): 1–182, 106–107 "We have been struck by the fact that the forgotten and repressed experiences of childhood are reproduced during the work of analysis in dreams and reactions, particularly in those occurring in the transference, although their revival runs counter to the interest of the pleasure principle; [...] There are people in whose lives the same reactions are perpetually being repeated uncorrected, to their own detriment, or others who seem to be pursued by a relentless fate, though closer investigation teaches us that they are unwittingly bringing this fate on themselves. In such cases we attribute a 'daemonic' character to the compulsion to repeat."

17 Cf. Chantraine, *Dictionnaire etymologique de la langue grecque: histoire des mots* (Paris: Librairie Klincksieck, 1999).

18 Sophocles, *Oedipus King of Thebes*, transl. G. Murray (Oxford: Oxford University Press, 1911), 872–876, 50 (https://archive.org/details/oedipuskingtheb00sophgoog/page/n72/mode/2up?q=pride). This comment from the Chorus is anticipated by a significant episode. We are at the point where Oedipus is about to receive from Apollo the foretelling that he will be guilty of incest and patricide. In verses 779-785, he relates that finding himself at a luncheon a drunken man calls him a bastard. Disdainful, he goes to his parents the next day to question them, and they are offended at those who have thus outraged them, ("and they rose in their pride / And smote the mocker...."): we find (in translation) the same fatal word (*mock*) that we have already examined in regard to Shakespeare's *Henry V*. Of course, yet another example of tragic irony, "the mocker" is both the drunk and Oedipus.

19 Cf. M. A. Kicey, "Road to Nowhere: The Mobility of Oedipus and the Task of Interpretation," 2014, *The American Journal of Philology* 135, no. 1: 29–55.

20 Cf. S. Freud, "The Question of Lay Analysis," *The Standard Edition of the Complete Psychological Works of Sigmund Freud* 20 (1926): 177–258, 256: "In psycho-analysis there has existed from the very first an inseparable bond between cure and research [...] Our analytic procedure is the only one in which this precious conjunction is assured".

21 Cf. R. Mancini, *La fragilità dello Spirito. Leggere Hegel per comprendere il mondo globale*.

22 Cf. F. Fornari, "Considerazioni sulla semiosi affettiva," *Rivista di Psicoanalisi* 23, no. 3 (1977): 347–371.

23 C. Ginzburg, (1979), "Clues: Roots of an Evidential Paradigm."

24 W. R. Bion, *Experiences in Groups and Other Papers*, (New York: Brunner-Routledge, 1961), 90. By "basic assumption" Bion means the mass functioning of a group pervaded by emotions of distress in modes of attack/escape, dependence or symbiosis. Such states hinder the pursuit, as a working group, of the stated goals.

25 Ibid.

26 Ibid.

27 Ibid.

28 Ibid., 173–174.

29 Cf. S. Freud, "Civilization and its Discontents." *The Standard Edition of the Complete Psychological Works of Sigmund Freud* 21 (1930): 57–146, 125: "fear of loss of love, 'social' anxiety [*Angst vor dem Liebesverlust, 'soziale' Angst*]".

30 W. R. Bion, *Transformations* (1965; London: Karnac, 1991), 38.

31 Cf. G. Civitarese, "The Concept of Time in Bion's 'A theory of thinking'", *The International Journal of Psychoanalysis* 100 (2019): 182–205.

32 F. Tustin, *Autism and Childhood Psychosis* [1972] (London: Routledge, 1995).

33 Cf. C. Ashbach, K. Fraley, J. L. Poulton, *Suffering and Sacrifice in the Clinical Encounter* (Bicester: Phoenix Publishing House, 2020).

34 A. Hitchcock, director, *Psycho* (USA, 1960).

35 W. R. Bion, *Learning from Experience* [1962]. (London: Routledge, 2019), 10–11, italics added.

36 Cf. W. R. Bion, "Attacks on Linking", [1959] 1967, in *Second Thoughts*, 93–109. What happens is a destruction of the psychic bonds that remain from experiences of positive relationships with others, and thus function as preconceptions that can be saturated by future contacts and thus become realizations. Bion impressively describes the moment of rupture. As if he had received "a stabbing attack from within'" the patient has "a violent, convulsive movement' of the body" (p 95–96). On the psychic level the same event corresponds to a "invisible-visual hallucination", i.e. a hallucination devoid of any sensory qualities, an event that only records the tearing of the psychic tissue. A fragment of non-experience is created. Something traumatic is produced in the subject, but without really being experienced, that is to say, without receiving personal meaning; in fact, a rupture, a mere void. Arrogance can be thought of as the "minimal" phenomenal, i.e. not yet overtly pathological, correlate of such an invisible inner catastrophe. We can see it as determined by an accentuation of the physiological "lack" (the negative) inherent in the fact of being a subject, which is expressed in the impossibility of ever being able to satiate desire. As such, even when it infects the community, it passes unnoticed. Perhaps this is what Hannah Arendt means by the concept of the "banality of evil": the manifestation of forms of "violence" that are (still) superficial and widespread.

37 W. R. Bion, *Learning from Experience*, 11.

38 Ibid.

39 W. R. Bion, *Attacks on Linking*, 109.

40 W. R. Bion, *Learning from Experience*, 11.

41 Cf. S. Freud, (1921) "Group Psychology and the Analysis of the Ego." *The Standard Edition of the Complete Psychological Works of Sigmund Freud* 18 (1921): 65–144, 74: "[An] unconscious, in which all that is evil in the human mind is contained as a predisposition".

42 W. R. Bion, *Second Thoughts*, 162.

43 F. Borgogno, *One Life Heals Another: Beginnings, Maturity, Outcomes of a Vocation* [2020], transl. A. Elgar (International Psychoanalytic Books, 2021), 23–24.

44 O. F. Kernberg, "Thirty Methods To Destroy The Creativity Of Psychoanalytic Candidates." *International Journal of Psychoanalysis* 77 (1996): 1031–1040.

45 Cf. D. M. Terman, "Self Psychology as a Shift Away from the Paranoid Strain in Classical Analytic Theory," *Journal of the American Psychoanalytic Association* 62, no. 6 (2014): 1005–1024, 1008: "I doubt Freud himself fully understood the moral dimension of his theory. [...] However, the effect of his construction is to create a locus of alien, destructive, asocial forces within each individual—an 'evil other'—embodied in the aggressive and destructive aspects of the id. This ultimately became the death instinct, as I will discuss later. Alongside this aggressive-destructive element, the other component of this 'evil other' is sexuality, conceptualized by Freud in terms of tension-seeking discharge".

46 Ibid., 1040.

47 O. F. Kernberg, "Institutional Problems of Psychoanalytic Education," *Journal of the American Psychoanalytic Association* 34 (1986): 799–834; Id., "Suicide Prevention for Psychoanalytic Institutes and Societies," *Journal of the American Psychoanalytic Association* 60 (2012): 707–719. On the crisis of psychoanalytic institutions, see also A. Ferro, *The New Analyst's Guide to the Galaxy: Questions About Contemporary Psychoanalysis* (Karnac, 2017).

48 O. F. Kernberg, "Institutional Problems of Psychoanalytic Education," *Journal of the American Psychoanalytic Association* 34 (1986): 799–834, 817.

49 Ibid., 825

50 Ibid., 806.

51 W. R. Bion, *A Memoir of the Future* (London: Karnac, 1991), 66.

52 Cf S. Freud ("New Introductory Lectures On Psycho-Analysis," *The Standard Edition of the Complete Psychological Works of Sigmund Freud* 22 (1933): 1–182): "We approach the id with analogies: we call it a chaos, a cauldron full of seething excitations." (1933], 73); he sees the unconscious as a region inhabited by "a mob, eager for enjoyment and destruction" (S. Freud, "My Contact with Josef Popper-Lynkeus," *The Standard Edition of the Complete Psychological Works of Sigmund Freud* 22 (1932): 217–224, 221); he explains that it is "the 'daemonic' power which produces the dream-wish and which we find at work in our unconscious." (S. Freud, "The Interpretation of Dreams."

The Standard Edition of the Complete Psychological Works of Sigmund Freud 4 (1900): 614), which comes into the open in the "immorality of [...] dreams" (ibid., 620),

53 Cf. Ricoeur, *Freud and Philosophy: An Essay on Interpretation*, transl. D. Savage (1965; New Haven, CT: Yale University Press, 1970), 32.

54 Cf. G. Civitarese, "Dora: The Postscripts," *The Italian Psychoanalytic Annual* 10 (2016): 79–95.

55 If the influence of Sophocles is obvious and stated—though Bion does not say that he wrote "On Arrogance" as a commentary on *Oedipus Rex*—other influences may be more subterranean. We do not know, for example, whether Bion has read it, but in summarizing the human condition of inauthenticity under the concept of *dejection*, M. Heidegger (*Being and Time*, [1927], transl. J. Stambaugh, (New York: State University of New York, 1996)) mentions a suggestively similar triad in §§ 35, 36 and 37: 'idle talk' (*Gerede*), 'curiosity' (*Neugier*), and 'ambiguity' (*Zweideutigkeit*).

56 R. Felski, *The Limits of Critique* (Chicago: The University of Chicago Press, 2015), 189.

57 J. Butler, *Subjects of Desire: Hegelian Reflections in Twentieth-Century France* (New York: Columbia University Press, 1987).

58 Cf. F. Gander, *Be With* (New York: New Directions Books, 2018), 14: "*You existed me* / [...] *when* / I *saw—as you would* / *never again* / *be revealed—you see me* / *as I would never* / *again be revealed*".

59 Cf. F. Falappa, *Il cuore della ragione. Dialettiche dell'amore e del perdono in Hegel.*

60 A still-young Freud, "Group Psychology and Ego Analysis," *The Standard Edition of the Complete Psychological Works of Sigmund Freud* 18 (1921): 65–144, 89) apparently was allergic to such interpretations. Thus he recalls his visit to Bernheim 1899: "I can remember even then feeling a muffled hostility to this tyranny of suggestion. When a patient who showed himself unamenable was met with the shout: 'What are you doing? *Vous vous contre-suggestionnez*', I said to myself that this was an evident injustice and an act of violence."

61 Cf. W. R. Bion, *On Arrogance*.

62 Like the phoenix, the scientistic self-misunderstanding of psychoanalysis denounced by J. Habermas (*Knowledge and Human Interest*, [1968], transl. J. J. Shapiro (Cambridge, UK: Polity Press, 1987)) is continually reborn from the ashes in the various fashionable attempts to reduce the psychic to the neurological. If it goes well, we return to Freud's *Project for a Scientific Psychology*, dated 1895.

63 Cf. Ricoeur, *Freud and Philosophy: An Essay on Interpretation*, Trasl. D. Savage (1965; New Haven, CT: Yale University Press, 1970), cited.

64 Cf. J. Benjamin, "Beyond Doer and Done to: An Intersubjective View of Thirdness," *The Psychoanalytic Quarterly* 73, no. 1 (2004): 5–46.

65 Cf. Freud, S. "My Contact with Josef Popper-Lynkeus," *The Standard Edition of the Complete Psychological Works of Sigmund Freud* 22 (1932): 217–224, 221–222: "Dream-distortion was the profoundest and most difficult problem of

dream life [...] My explanation of dream-distortion seemed to me new: I had nowhere found any thing like it."

66 Cf. S. Freud, "Observations on Transference-Love (Further Recommendations on the Technique of Psycho-Analysis III)," *The Standard Edition of the Complete Psychological Works of Sigmund Freud* 12 (1915):157–171, 164.

67 R. Barthes, *The Neutral: Lecture Course at the College De France (1977-1978)*, 2002, transl. R. E. Krauss and D. Hollier (New York: Columbia University Press, 2007), 36: "Sweetness is the final word of Skepticism".

68 Ibid., R. Barthes, *The Neutral* 152.

69 Ibid., 157: "But Nietzsche is obviously the one who best dismantled {*a démonté*} (in both senses of the term) the concept ('On Truth and Falsity'): 'Every idea originates through equating the unequal', → thus concept: a force that reduces the diverse, the becoming that is the sensible, the *aisthèsis*".

70 Cf. W. R. Bion, *Cogitations* (London: Karnac, 1992).

71 G. W. F. Hegel, *The Phenomenology of Spirit*, 108 "What will later come to be for consciousness will be the experience of what spirit is, this absolute substance which constitutes the unity of its oppositions in their complete freedom and self-sufficiency, namely, in the oppositions of the various self-consciousnesses existing for themselves: The *I* that is *we* and the *we* that is *I*. Consciousness has its turning point in self-consciousness, as the concept of spirit, where, leaving behind the colorful semblance of the this-worldly sensuous, and leaving behind the empty night of the super- sensible other-worldly beyond, it steps into the spiritual daylight of the present."

72 H. Schwartz, "Barthes, the Neutral, and our neutrality", *American Imago* 70, no. 3 (2013): 487–513, 495: "With the Neutral (a word he always capitalizes) Barthes aimed at the curious task of reaching a domain outside the opposition and conflict of differences that we require to make meaning. He called it a 'seeking,' a 'striving,' and a 'desire'— 'the desire for Neutral'—that could only be captured in 'twinklings' and 'shimmerings. This entails: '-first: suspension (*epoché*) of orders, laws, summons, arrogance, terrorisms, puttings on notice, the will-to-possess. -then, by way of deepening, refusal of pure discourse of opposition. Suspension of narcissism'".

73 R. Barthes, *The Neutral*, 153.

74 Ibid., 95.

75 Cf. Y. Citton, "La nuance contre l'arrogance. Lectures croisées entre Roland Barthes et Gilles Deleuze", in *Empreintes de Roland Barthes*, ed. D. Bougnoux, (Paris: INA, 2009), 147–183.

Chapter 3

Arrogance and Society

3.1 Doxa

What is the legitimacy, and usefulness, of calling ours the "civilization of arrogance?" Why not, for example, stick to Lasch's[1] famous characterization of the "culture of narcissism", Bauman's[2] "liquid modernity", Augé's[3] "non-place", Lyotard's[4] "postmodernity", Marcuse's[5] "one-dimensional" society of men, or Ternynck's[6] "men of sand?" All these terms, which come from critical theory, philosophy, and sociology, partly overlap, they capture similar phenomena. The same is true of the one I propose in these pages, but together they form a new vertex of observation. Ideally, as Mancini hopes, it could compete with the others mentioned above to form an integrated critical theory.

However, there is a difference: the concepts of non-place, postmodernism, narcissism, one-dimensionality, and liquid society are mainly aimed at describing the social phenomena of late capitalism and globalization. The concept of arrogance, on the other hand, seems to have a double valence: it is more descriptive, that is to say, it is aimed at actuality, and, from a psychoanalytic point of view, it is explanatory in the sense of genetic causality. On the one hand, it lends itself to the characterization of some salient aspects of contemporaneity; on the other hand, relying on the capacity of psychoanalysis to postulate an essential isomorphism between the individual and the collective psyche, it functions as a penetrating key to understanding the concept of *hýbris*, a theoretical parameter that sums up and defines the entire history and culture of the West.[7]

To this end, after that of "neutral", I take my cue from another of Barthes' concepts, "doxa", which highlights the nexus between individual psychology and social psychology. The realm of doxa, and the elective place where the symptoms of the civilization of arrogance are most evident, are

DOI: 10.4324/9781032669427-4

the media. Barthes uses this term to refer to the power that mass culture, popular opinion, or common sense exerts over the individual. Doxa has such power because it is based on what is taken for granted and as such is never questioned. Doxa succeeds in transforming what is merely contingent into something natural. Like Medusa, the doxa "petrifies those who look at her", it is "a gelatinous mass that sticks onto the retina".[8] It stops you from thinking, it literally makes you stupid. A current example is the system of *likes* in social media. As long as something or someone receives a lot of them, the popularity index guarantees its value. As Pierrot[9] writes, "While the voice of doxa is imperious and arrogant, like that of the militant or of Science, its mode of diffusion is insidious". In the words of Barthes,[10] "The Doxa is not triumphalist; it is content to reign; it diffuses, blurs; it is a legal, a natural dominance; a general layer, spread with the blessing of Power; a universal Discourse, a mode of jactancy which is already lurking in the mere fact of 'holding' a discourse (upon something): whence the natural affinity between endoxal discourse and radiophony".

Democracy itself is interpreted as the arrogance of the doxa, when one imagines being able to bypass the complex function of mediating representativeness guaranteed by parliament in the exercise of direct and absolute power—essentially to tick off a "like". It would be a form of mass tyranny, of course, and the availability of cyberspace would make it possible.

But the single word most often associated with the noun "arrogance" and the adjective "arrogant" is "power". Typically, this happens when the exercise of power loses its ideal purpose of serving the community that expressed it and becomes self-referential. Power declines mainly as political power and as economic-financial power. In order to defend itself against the omnipresence of the latter, the former takes on anti-democratic, populist, and nationalist accents. To maintain itself and regain ground, it borrows the aggressive advertising techniques that the economic-financial power has already developed for marketing. In a bewildering confusion of roles, even politics is bending to the logic of the audience. Selling more or increasing the electoral consensus, and thus power, becomes an objective completely divorced from the social rationality that would like to see an ethical principle at the heart of politics. An idea is sold in the same way as a brand of coffee. The unifying element is "selling", or more precisely, in most cases, "telesales".

Everything that escapes the numbers of the audience is banished from this world. Only what can be simplified into slogans can be said. The justification is circular. Revenues, whether economic or political, are increased.

The success of the method confirms that this is the only point of view worth considering. Existence itself is digitalized, and the meaning of life is reduced to the dichotomous logic of the binary numerical system, which allows only two digits. The world is ruled by dualism, an inherently violent principle because it offers only the choice between chatter and silence.

Bion[11] opens the first page of the fourth chapter of *Transformations* by asking whether analysts are "painters" or propagandists. Both work on the emotions of the patient or of the audience, but with different purposes. The propagandist has something to sell, his purpose is not to make his audience more free, but to enslave them to a product. To do this, he uses the emotions he arouses in them to manipulate them. The painter who is an authentic artist, on the other hand, is not primarily concerned with selling anything, but only with touching his audience emotionally. The analyst works with a patient's emotions by giving a verbal representation of them, just as a painter gives a visual representation of his subject with canvas and colors. And it could be an interpretation formulated in a session, but it could also be a scientific publication. In both cases, it would be a verbal representation of an emotional experience.

It is banal to remember it, but in our culture almost everything is advertising. The pervasiveness and insidiousness of advertising on the Internet has reached the intolerable level of a real colonization of the mind. The possibility, each time you visit a site on the Internet, to give your consent to the service files that record your access and to choose between different options, is in fact fictitious and contrary to the very spirit of the Internet and of "surfing" on the Net. A mere legalistic trick. Its only effect, sadly and ironically, is to remind us that we have already given up any privacy. The mocking procedure is repeated endlessly, a parody of a principle of civilization which would be to have the last word on how much and which part of one's most intimate life should be alienated. This new form of servitude is particularly evident when we are offered to buy products that we have not researched, but that some algorithm has associated with words abusively extracted from our private communications. It is called "behavioral advertising". Behavioral targeting sounds even more disturbing because people are assimilated into so many "targets".

I won't even mention the collective arrogance with which we approach ecological issues and the systematic destruction of natural habitats. This social pathology has become so obvious that it is now officially on the political agenda. But that doesn't mean that solutions are at hand.

Corporate culture is being grafted onto the management of health care, one of the privileged sites of biopolitics. The choice is justified by the "perfectly rational" need for prudent management of resources. As a result, the public health system is usually subjected to the double logic of profit and politics reduced to power.

In the field of health care that I know best, that of the treatment of mental illness, the rise of the ideology of cognitivism is a symptom of the triumph of the paradigm of technique. In psychiatry, on the one hand, it is the uncritical return, with the various diagnostic-statistical manuals, to the spirit of Kraepelin and, on the other, to a desperate biologism. Diagnosis and psychotropic drugs are good in themselves if they are part of an integrated perspective of care in which the value of the relationship is kept alive. On the contrary, they become instruments of alienation when they humiliate existence and fail to consider the multifactorial nature (of a bio-psycho-social order, as they say) involved in the etiopathogenesis of mental suffering. Hamlet's dilemma, if his classic monologue were updated for today, "to be autonomous or automated?" As Marcuse[12] announced as early as 1964, technological rationality has become political rationality. And one might add: totalitarian oppression has been exchanged for covert persuasion, contradiction for neurosis. But from the windows shines "A comfortable, smooth, reasonable, democratic unfreedom".[13] Never as now the collective dream is the abolition of work thanks to automation. The side effect could be the "abolition" of the individual, now deprived of the dignity that comes from work and reduced to a consumer or desiring machine.

People wake up in the morning and start stuffing their heads with SPREAD, ECB, GDP, G5, G7, G20, etc. From the top of their capital letters, the acronyms mock their insignificant existence as ants of capital. The improvement of material living conditions, i.e., the growth of productivity at any cost has become an end in itself. It doesn't matter if in the meantime we pay for it in terms of exploitation, pollution, greater inequality with less developed countries. The time of life is marked by economic cycles, the quarterly reports of large multinationals, and the meetings of central banks, whose presidents have become the modern oracles.

But they themselves are cogs in the system. When the new President of the European Central Bank took office and made a gaffe, the world turned on her until she retracted almost everything she had just said. The system provides rules and assigns roles, but no one can really see themselves as being in a position to deal cards. The whole world of economics looks like a top gone mad. If it slows down or stops, everything collapses. The logic of abstraction prevents us from seeing that the well-being of A is paid for by the unhappiness of B—not because B has not yet reached the well-being of A, but because his unhappiness is functional to that well-being. The same logic conceals the fact that you are consuming more goods, but in the meantime, the sea and the air you remember from your childhood are no longer the same, so you have to plan your holidays elsewhere, and in the meantime, you start watching the advertisements. Then, you realize that you don't have time to visit the website of one of these holiday resorts, and that you are being inundated with a series of offers that are becoming more and more insidious and insistent.

Even with the commercial agencies that provide you with services and should at least treat you with the respect due to clients, the relationship tends to become more and more impersonal, in the name of subservience and anonymity. No longer customers, but clients reduced to numbers, little more than things, assets. Why should a major national insurance company, whose policies I have subscribed to for decades, call me on my mobile phone on a summer's day to persuasively suggest that I buy their latest product? If that's not "arrogance", what is?

Staying on this ground, I'd like to mention the COVID-19 pandemic[14] by adopting the fiction that it was some sort of laboratory "experiment" to study the discomfort of modern civilization.

3.2 Pandemic

The COVID-19 epidemic represents a kind of worldwide "test" of the new political-health order. The pandemic perfectly realizes a split within society between security reasons and spiritual needs. Citizens agree to give up their fundamental rights in the name of the health emergency. Governments proclaim the suspension of democracy and the state of exception becomes the normal state. According to some, we live in a climate of "health terror".[15] Never before have we been forced by law to behave as if we really were completely isolated from one another. It is solipsism realized. The watchword is "social distancing". Paranoia is elected as a moral obligation and practice of life. I am invited to see in my fellow man a potential unctor. Even the family member who does not respect the rules and gets infected could be the saboteur who ruins the house. I, in turn, am a danger to others and must be monitored with such intrusive devices that Bentham's

Panopticon, an ideal prison, makes one smile; one in which the forms of social control devised in the ex-communist states of Eastern Europe pale, and Foucault's[16] "discipline and punish" seems obsolete.

On the one hand, we've ended up like the human beings in *The Matrix*,[17] each stuffed into their own pods and kept in a vegetative life (the vegetative life of the consumer) to supply the system with energy. Thanks to the new digital technologies the new State-as-Leviathan controls individuals in a capillary and extremely intrusive way. If it implies transgression of the new order based on "social distancing", satisfying the most basic affective needs is benned. Dramatically, the outcome to be avoided at all costs, the rows of beds with intubated patients in intensive care units, is allegorically prefigured by the disciplinary device that is supposed to exorcise it. In fact, people are in fact reduced to living in special niches of cyberspace. Isolated but connected and happy followers of the cult of online shopping.

Constituted power sweeps mismanagement and commercial exploitation of health care under the rug of emergency. Such a society, however, is not free. Under these conditions a life is not worth living. Humanity is brought back to biology, while any political or social dimensions are reduced to zero. Of course, the question is not about the measures needed to overcome the pandemic, nor can it be said that it was governments that created it. Rather, the question is whether and how it may be exploited for the mere perpetuation of power; and what happens when a functional split becomes pathological.[18]

For Agamben,[19] the new religion of science, and especially of medicine, establishes a kind of new technological totalitarianism in the name of dogmatic theology that opposes disease or the virus (equated with absolute Evil) to health or healing (Good). As citizens, we are all reduced to practitioners of this cult. The incessant prayer is to keep ourselves "separate and at a distance". A new phenomenology of the mass becomes thus visible, but of "a mass, so to speak, overturned, formed by individuals who keep themselves at a distance from one another at all costs [...] a rarefied mass based on a prohibition, but, precisely for this reason, particularly compact and passive".

Agamben again points out that epidemic comes from *demos* (people) and that in Homer *polemos epidemios* is civil war: "All nations and all peoples are now permanently at war with themselves, because the invisible and elusive enemy with whom they are fighting is within us".[20] It is easy to see that it is as if we were guinea pigs in a cruel project that could be called "construction of disciplinary regimes in the field of biopolitical devices".

We hope that these are temporary measures, but of course we all suspect that the dress rehearsal of our near future is underway. It is easy to presume that once the pandemic has passed, the paradigm that expresses it will persist, if not the literal state of exception. Now based on health (on the spread of "health terror"), even more effectively than on the fight against terrorism, it will justify an unprecedented and "invisible" type of health-technological despotism whose ideological framework consists of the new cult dedicated to the gods of Science (or rather of Medicine) and consumerism (or money). Health is no longer a right but a legal obligation to be fulfilled at all costs.[21]

The ability of technology to intrude into the lives of others, i.e., our own, and to implement widespread control, has grown so exponentially that we struggle to be aware of it. Drones, smart control, task forces, cookies, facial recognition cameras, apps that track our movements, tourists are required not only to show their ID cards but also to submit to body temperature checks, etc. Ostensibly, all these devices are designed to protect health and privacy (which itself should be seen as a form of mental health), but in fact they become tools for systematic profiling.. Here life is either "hygienic" (or capitalist) or it is not. It is the permanent sanitization of bodies, of affects, of sociality: of all that escapes the magnificent and progressive fates of technocracy and science, all aspects that fall under what Derrida calls "the globalization of avowal".[22]

If these are some of the easily visible forms of alienation in the contemporary world, those in which a dramatic split occurs between abstract logic and reason, then the question then is always the same: can we identify an origin, a cause, a principle? Could the concept of arrogance/*hýbris*, as we have configured and questioned it, be a kind of common denominator for all these manifestations? What does psychoanalysis have to say as a critical theory when starting from Freud, but integrating it with the subsequent developments of the discipline he founded, it tries to reflect on the "new" malaise of civilization?

3.3   The New Malaise of Civilization

Although written by Freud in 1929, *Civilization and Its Discontents* remains a precious legacy to read the present, an extraordinary meditation on the possibility that human beings have to be happy or, on the contrary, on unhappiness and therefore evil. Freud wrote the essay in order to refute the objection raised by Romain Rolland against his conception of religion. We are therefore on the ground of ethics. Rolland rejects Freud's reductionism and argues that religion channels the "oceanic feeling" of man. As a true enlightener, Freud does not really grasp the meaning of this intuition and lets it fall badly.

Today, however, without abandoning the terrain of psychology, we would more easily translate oceanic feeling with "intersubjectivity" in the Husserlian sense of the community that transcends the individual and makes its birth possible. We would acknowledge Freud for preparing the ground for this concept so central to the culture of the last century and to our own by inventing/discovering the unconscious, but we would no longer think that it can be easily refuted as if it were a mere illusion.

Freud anticipates but does not develop, the concept of intersubjectivity. He postulates in the infant an initial phase of indistinction of the ego from the object-environment or "of unlimited narcissism", of being "at one" with the whole, and that therefore it can remain in some way as a residue in psychic life. However, he then theorizes that separation from it occurs as a result of efforts to remove painful internal and external stimuli in a unidirectional sense, so to speak. In this way he does not consider that the detachment of the ego from the external world can only come about through another kind of "more intimate bond"[23] with the other, i.e. a going out into the world, which is realised through language and which, like subjectivity, remains a dimension that is always necessary in order to be able to speak of a subject and consequently of having an "object" before one's eyes.

Freud admits only as an exception, in psychotic pathology and in falling in love, that the "clear and sharp lines of demarcation"[24] of the ego can dissolve, into two human conditions, each unique in itself but of opposite signs. But from our point of view, it is now easy to see that the exception is the rule. Normally invisible, the network of libidinal bonds that makes the unity of collective formations is always active. Freud himself at one point felt the need to postulate the concept of Eros. More comprehensive than the libido as a sexual drive, Eros represents a principle of bonding "whose purpose is to combine single human individuals, and after that families, then races, peoples and nations, into one great unity, the unity of mankind".[25] The libido is, therefore, only a tool at the disposal of Eros in the pursuit of its aims. It is clear that, in this context, the death instinct (aggression) could be seen as an instinct, albeit an anti-libidinal instinct, i.e., one aimed at limiting the tendency of the group to merge, or as the work of the negative.

Significantly, in *Civilization and Its Discontents,* the struggle between Eros and Thanatos comes to resemble more and more the struggle between master and servant according to Hegel, although Freud seems to see them not in a relationship of antagonistic solidarity but of clear opposition. However, if we read the relationship between Eros and Thanatos in this way, as a way of conceiving the dialectic that leads to the development of self-consciousness, it is easier for us to see the weaknesses in Freud's text and to relativize his concepts of aggression and sexuality, which are otherwise regarded as primary drives. Let's look at one first, then the other.

Faced with the horrors of the war that has just ended, and with a foreboding of the one that is to come, Freud feels the need to hypothesize, purely theoretically, as he insists, the existence of a death drive. A primary and unquenchable instinct of aggression forever marks the destiny of man. This drive is the source of the most pernicious impulses which give rise to wars, violence, and various forms of cruelty. Since it is primary, i.e., immediate, the aggressiveness of man cannot be eliminated. It can only be curbed at the cost of a kind of costly immunization. Part of the aggression is internalized as the superego or moral consciousness, and turning against the ego limits its destructiveness.

It seems to escape Freud that there is something contradictory in the way he tries to articulate the relationship between the two terms of the death instinct and the development of moral consciousness. According to this logic, language would have developed to contain primary aggression, but then animals could certainly not be imagined to be "happier" than human beings. Nor would we speak of primary aggression (of nature), since nature is the only dimension in which they live. In this respect, they seem to be freer than men, but they have constraints that are unknown to men. Nor would we think of processes of internalization of parental norms, since, strictly speaking, animals have no world, or are "poor in the world",[26] before them, since they have no language". So if humans have a death drive, it is by definition not to be confused with the instinct of aggression. In fact, Freud writes *Trieb*, not *Instinkt*. As a concept, the drive is to be considered already human, it belongs to the field of the symbolic and therefore has always been "social". It cannot be argued that since there is primary aggression and we want civilization at all costs, then we must pay the price of repressing the instinct.

Without civilization, what would still be a mere instinct, and not a drive, would not need to be removed. Rather, aggression (violence) and repression are in a relationship of mutual implication and are not linked by the linear processuality envisaged by Freud. The Freudian unconscious is based on repression, and repression, as censorship, is itself an act of violence. From the beginning, both are elements of the human landscape. There is no drive without repression (civilization) and vice versa. What is repressed is not the primary violence but, if anything, the violence that the act of repression itself liberates.

The essential aspect to grasp is that there is no humanity (thought, self-consciousness) without language, and that language already has a normative character in itself. It is as if by "civilization" Freud meant the symbolic and then made a leap outside this sphere by proposing the explanation of primary aggression. But this leap cannot be made. It is as if he were hypothesizing a direct, unmediated line of connection between words and things. But there can be no civilization or self-consciousness without the "violence" inherent in language. There would be no order and there would be no language. Language is necessary for order and violence, and the drive, even when it expresses itself in the individual, is still to be regarded as social.

Consequently, when Freud states that man has an innate tendency "to 'badness', to aggressiveness and destructiveness, and so to cruelty as well",[27] one could logically also assert the opposite, that is, that he has a deep moral nature and a spontaneous inclination to the good. Good and evil are not absolutes but are principles of ethical life, born *together* with the birth of ethical life. It is therefore problematic to argue that human aggression is primary, as if it existed before self-consciousness, or secondary, as if it arose out of frustration, but also thought outside the domain of language. If it was a language that unleashed sexuality and aggression, how could they be "primary"? If the death drive, as Freud writes, offers to the ego the fulfillment of its "old wishes for omnipotence",[28] should we then think that omnipotence is also "an original, self-subsisting instinctual disposition in man"?[29] On the contrary, the introjection of aggression as moral consciousness—or "or more correctly", as Freud specifies, "the anxiety which later becomes conscience"[30] and guilt—shows its indispensable balancing function. Freud writes that civilization "obtains mastery" in this way "over the individual's dangerous desire for aggression",[31] as if this were an entirely avoidable and incidental factor. But without aggression, there would not even be civilization, or even the mere possibility any kind of "desire" being constituted. The two terms can only coexist; all the more so since, as Freud points out, guilt exists independently of evil.

Something similar is theorized by René Girard. As Mancini[32] points out: "If in taking up the Freudian lesson it is possible to hypothesize a death drive that structures the relationship between nature and culture, with René Girard the center of attention shifts from the biological sphere to the social sphere. On the contrary, the current of violence that, according to the French scholar, runs through every culture represents what is structurally and universally social, insofar as it constitutes the foundation of the order of living together. *It is not society that produces violence, but violence that produces society*".

This statement should be corrected: society and violence are co-born to each other in a dialectical and mutually generative relationship. Similarly, Fromm[33] gives a historical and social interpretation of the death drive and destructive aggression as a reaction to frustration, and therefore essentially secondary. Foucault[34] also agrees with Freud's "error": "Freud, in advancing in the direction of the relation between desire and truth, was mistaken; he thought that Oedipus was speaking to him about the universal forms of desire, whereas, in a lowered voice, the Oedipus fable was recounting to him the historical constraint weighing on our system of truth, on that system to which Freud himself belonged".

According to Freud[35] "men are not gentle creatures who want to be loved, and who at the most can defend themselves if they are attacked; they are, on the contrary, creatures among whose instinctual endowments is to be reckoned a powerful share of aggressiveness". However, we would do the same for animals by invoking the instinct and therefore the non-consciousness and the absence of guilt. But then it is self-consciousness that makes man guilty; not trivially in the sense of making him aware of a guilt that was already there, but in the sense of creating it for the first time. In fact, the self-consciousness made possible by the acquisition of language is the only thing that differentiates us from animals. In animals, there is no guilt because there is no responsibility. Therefore, the ego does not reveal a fault that was already there but carries it with it as its shadow.

Reversing the argument, we could say that it is the fault (the norm) or the sense of responsibility toward the other that creates the Ego. In this sense, we say that we come into the world with original sin. The sense of good and evil does not pre-exist to the subject but it is consubstantial to him. When Freud speaks of an instinctual aggressiveness that is primary, original, animal, he disregards the factor of language as the basis of self-consciousness. It follows that he makes guilt or evil independent of the plane of human intersubjectivity (the "oceanic feeling"). From this angle, venting one's aggression would be tantamount to letting this cruel drive aggression run rampant. It is no coincidence that it is at this point in *Civilization and Its Discontents* that Freud lists some of the worst crimes of which man can be guilty.

But if we come to see human aggression as an invention of civilization, and if we can no longer follow Freud's line of thought, which, I repeat, consists of explaining man on the basis of a factor that is in itself extra-human, merely natural—that is to say, which cannot be considered specifically human, because then it would have to be read not with the concept of drive but with that of instinct—nevertheless, starting from the moment when this aggression is *awakened*, the description of the psychic dynamics to which it gives rise remains perfectly acceptable. In short, the cause of human unhappiness may not be what Freud thinks it is. Yet we are persuaded by the way he schematizes the process that leads to the constitution of moral consciousness, which, when it becomes cruel, ultimately produces psychic suffering. From this perspective, then, evil as unnecessary violence, as opposed to necessary violence, would not be something intrinsic to mere nature or civilization, but rather a perversion of it. What Freud calls the "untying" of the life instinct and the death instinct would correspond to a change in the dialectic between identity and difference, or identification and dis-identification (negation).

All of *Civilization and Its Discontents* is therefore pervaded by an essential ambivalence. Freud seems to adopt a resigned and pessimistic position. However, when faced with the question of whether civilization is fatally opposed to happiness, in the eighth and final chapter he discusses the superego, which he defines as "a garrison in a conquered city",[36] and delves into the unconscious relational dynamics from which it emerges. Thus, in contrast to the inevitability of nature, Freud introduces the plasticity of culture and therefore the role of the environment. Not only constitutional factors are at stake, but also environmental influences. The "experience of being loved"[37] plays a decisive role in deflecting inward the aggressiveness that arises from drive frustration, and thus in deciding the quality of moral consciousness. It is significant that Freud relegates this expression to a footnote—a choice for which one could speak of a return effect of the repressed. Similarly, it is noteworthy that he toned down the dramatic emphasis of the essay's title by substituting "discomfort" (*Unbehagen*) for "unhappiness" (*Unglück*).

Evil ("what is bad") is transformed from innate cruelty into "whatever causes one to be threatened with loss of love",[38] that is, external and internal "punitive aggression".[39] The aggression directed against the self of the moral instance serves to dodge the aggression that would be inferred from the loss of the object. You can see how Freud gradually arrives at a dialectical rather than a dichotomous logic. Except for a fleeting mention of "innate constitutional factors",[40] he surprisingly seems to forget about the death drive and instead leads everything back to the dynamics of the primary relationship. In the end, amidst somewhat confused or mythical references to the primitive horde and to the murder of the father, etc., Freud admits the essential: "Since civilization obeys an internal erotic impulsion which causes human beings to unite in a closely-knit group, it can only achieve this aim through an ever-increasing reinforcement of the sense of guilt".[41]

3.4 Scientia Sexualis

We find the same basic misunderstanding in Freud about the repression of sexuality. He gives the impression of dreaming of a kind of Eden, which then—again—could only coincide with the animal state, and in which there would be a completely free sexuality. But the "sexuality" that we know, like human aggression, is *also* an invention of civilization. Animals reproduce, we cannot say that they have a sexuality. On the contrary, civilization, which must regulate its subversive aspects, as the sphere of maximum emotional and/or physical intimacy in which the subject plays the game of recognition, has certainly freed sexuality from the bonds of biology. Beyond the essential fact, pure and simple, of inaugurating a new form of life, it has allowed it to expand enormously in its extrinsications. And among these, for example, is the whole sphere that Freud ascribes to sublimation.

When Freud states that civilization tends to limit sexual life, it is hard to see what the term of comparison is. There have been and there are societies with different degrees of sexual freedom, but sexuality is invariably present in all of them. Nor would it be easy to compare and evaluate different societies with respect to this parameter without falling into an ideological vision. The basic misunderstanding is to contrast the discomfort of civilization with some kind of utopian rule. In fact, we know that from Moro to Campanella,[42] at least as far as the best-known utopias invented by men are concerned, they are always totalitarian universes. So, Freud sees the taboo

of incest not as a prerequisite for the invention of sexuality, but as a renun-
ciation of the exercise of a freedom that has never really existed, unless we
want to believe in mythologies of primitives and earthly paradises. In fact,
Freedom presupposes an effective possibility of choice.

For Freud,[43] freedom is not the product of civilization, but civilization results from the limitation of freedom: "civilization behaves towards sexuality
as a people or a stratum of its population does which has subjected another
one to its exploitation. Fear of a revolt by the suppressed elements drives it
to stricter precautionary measures". The metaphor here is very clear. There
is a relationship of exploitation between civilization and sexuality. But then
the ego exploits the id? The conscious the unconscious? Didn't we say that
the Ego is not the master in its own house? Who exploits whom?

Obviously, the fact that civilization has freed sexuality from the strict
constraints of instinct does not mean that sexuality, as a field in which the
'mortal' struggle for recognition takes place, does not retain something subversive. These constraints have been replaced by others, but much looser
ones. The image of the exploitative relationship here could be read in the
light of the master/servant relationship described by Hegel as a stage prior
to mutual recognition and thus to a situation of reconciliation. I mean that
neither aggression nor sexuality can be conceptualized in the abstract, outside the system of dynamic equilibria within which they take shape and
manifest themselves. Aggression and sexuality are not destructive per se,
but only when they arise from the crisis of this system; in essence, from
the prevalence of splitting logics that corrupt the dialectic *Ego/Es*, *C/Unc*,
subjectivity/intersubjectivity, abstract rationality/affective body.

Freud clearly denounces sexual repression and advocates greater sexual
freedom. However, his position is ultimately ambiguous for another reason.
The summit of observation is essentially that of a psychology of the isolated subject. Freud contrasts the individual and civilization (social group)
as two completely separate entities. He does not put himself in the perspective of a social field in which the individual and the other/group are in a dialectical relationship, and in which the question to be asked would be how
much freedom a given society as a whole can tolerate without falling apart.
The point is not to isolate tensions as existing between different poles, but
instead to see them as internal to the same dynamic field of forces. Freud's
position is also ambiguous because on the one hand, he wants to reduce the
damage caused by sexual repression, while on the other hand, he continues
to identify sexuality and the "sexual lusts"[44] of the "savage beast",[45] going

so far as to say that sexuality sometimes gives him "the impression of being in process of involution as a function".[46]

On this point, I believe that Foucault's critique of psychoanalysis deserves the utmost attention (even if it must be accepted with some reservations) when he declares that he does not claim to deny that sexuality is repressed, but that the issue of suppression/repression must be addressed within the framework of a more complex, a more global strategy of power and domination relations in society. For Foucault, it is power (but a power that should be thought of as diffuse, pervasive, anonymous, plural, elusive, and mobile) that generates around sexuality a discourse or regime of truth that serves to legitimize and proliferate it. It is obvious how: new caesuras are created between normal and abnormal, pure and impure, licit and illicit. Power, as it were, is not interested in erasing sexuality, quite the contrary. The more sexuality there is, the more prohibitions there are, and a whole new restrictive economy develops. Not censorship, then, but since the eighteenth century "a kind of generalized discursive heretism",[47] "a veritable discursive explosion",[48] capable of functioning and producing effects on the forms of life related to the expression of sexuality. Sex becomes the concern of the police, morality, biology, medicine, and psychology.

Coming to contemporary times, with regard to the proliferation of the discourse on sexuality, Marcuse[49] uses the Freudian category of sublimation, which he paradoxically praises, since it would preserve the memory of the repression that produced it, and consequently also the impulse toward liberation, and turns it into that of repressive "desublimation". Again, according to this author, sexuality would only be falsely liberated. It is liberalized but in controlled and socially constructive forms that realize new relations of domination. More sexuality, yes, but reduced to the level of mere instinctual gratification. The self-transcendence of the libido, its outpouring "beyond the immediate erotogenic zones"[50] (*sic*) is thus depotentiated. What matters is instead that alienation feeds the unhappy conscience, and thus the desire to revolt against the misdeeds of society and its 'reality principle'.

Reread today, these pages do not lose much of their argumentative force, but at times they also sound a bit naive, for example when Marcuse[51] contrasts commodified sex with "love-making in a meadow and in an automobile, on a lovers' walk outside the town walls and on a and on a Manhattan street", or when he takes issue with sexuality in the world, or when[52] he takes issue with the sexuality of a woman, or he takes issue with the "desublimated sexuality is rampant in O'Neill's alcoholics and Faulkner's savages, in the *Streetcar Named Desire* and under the *Hot Tin Roof*, in *Lolita*", and so on.

However, despite the inevitably dated aspects of his ideas, his diagnosis of the one-track mind, calculating, absolute, where there is only one vision of life, remains effective as a representation of the arrogant imprint of a society that presents only one and only one dimension of existence and personal fulfillment. The champion of such a society, according to Marcuse, is the advertising agent. The sore point of advertising is that the discourse in which it is embodied "is deprived of the mediations which are the stages of the process of cognition and cognitive evaluation [...] Without these mediations, language tends to express and promote the immediate identification of reason with fact, truth and established truth, essence and existence, the thing, and its function".[53] The discourse goes only and always in the same direction, expressing authoritarian instances and proceeding through hypnotic formulas and subtly "intimidating" tautologies. In short, Marcuse illustrates the "overwhelming *concreteness*" of the language of arrogance, which "creates a basic vocabulary and syntax which stand in the way of differentiation, separation, and distinction [...] irreconcilably anti-critical and anti-dialectical".[54]

For Foucault, these new scenarios of sexuality are not produced as a result of the removal of a prohibition, but rather as a result of an increasingly pervasive annexation of bodies and souls to power. The real prohibition would now concern the possibility of *not* talking about sex. At the same time, the more we talk about it, the more we turn it into something that lives in the sphere of secrecy. The last two centuries writes Foucault, "have been rather the age of multiplication: a dispersion of sexualities, a strengthening of their disparate forms, a multiform settlement of 'perversions.' Our epoch has initiated sexual heterogeneities"[55] of "peripheral",[56] "scattered",[57] "unorthodox [...] disparate"[58] sexualities. Hence the centrality of perversion in this particular order of discourse. It is on the perverse sexuality, on the "aberrations, perversions, exceptional oddities, pathological abatements, and morbid aggravations",[59] that the multiplication and the ramification of sexuality and of the norms that sanction it are based. What links us to the theme of arrogance/*hýbris* and the search for truth at any cost, the obsessive scrutiny of sexuality, the new *scientia sexualis*, comes to participate in the "immense will to knowledge that has sustained the establishment of scientific discourse in the West".[60]

In the list of agencies that help to define the field of this science, Foucault does not hesitate to include, in addition to medicine and psychiatry, psychoanalysis itself and its ability to annex the procedure of confession by inventing and prescribing free association to the patient and fluctuating or evenly suspended attention to the analyst. Freud's tactical decision is to weave a whole web of sexual causation of neurosis: "By no longer making the confession a test, but rather a sign, and by making sexuality something to be interpreted, the nineteenth century gave itself the possibility of causing the procedures of confession to operate within the regular formation of a scientific discourse".[61] *It is not a question of punishing but of deciphering, decoding, and diagnosing.*

Psychoanalysis itself would be part of the mechanisms of adaptation to the various existing regimes of domination. The tools it uses—"the listening technique, the postulate of causality, the principle of latency, the rule of interpretation, the imperative of medicalization"[62]—make it a hermeneutic of suspicion. It would like to be an *ars erotica*, but it ends up being only, in fact, a *scientia sexualis*, even if Foucault also considers the hypothesis that the latter can be configured as a particularly subtle form of the former.

In essence, entirely in line with the reinvention of the Oedipus that Bion places at the center of his essay on arrogance, we are no longer dealing with a repressive regime of sexuality, but with a "'political economy' of a will to knowledge",[63] with the *hýbris* of "an never-ending demand for truth",[64] and with "a formidable *petition to know*".[65] For Foucault, the fact that civilization cannot be founded on the repression of sexuality and aggression according to linear and unidirectional logic is quite obvious: "one should not think that desire is repressed, for the simple reason that the law is what constitutes both desire and the lack on which it is predicated. Where there is desire, the power relation is already present"; it is illusory, then, to denounce "this relation for a repression exerted after the event".[66]

Freud's ambiguity, I repeat, lies entirely in his use of the term "drive" (*Trieb*), with which he seeks to resolve the link between nature and culture. In fact, by inventing this concept, he merely reformulates the problem by giving it a hypothetical definition. As an instinct, *libido* would have nothing to do with culture, and would therefore be prior to it. As a drive, it would be part of it to all intents and purposes. According to Foucault, the repression of sexuality perpetrated by laws, rules, and codes may be evident, but not by a certain kind of knowledge about sex or 'technology' of sex, which he instead calls 'power'. Not an institution or a structure but a "complex strategical situation".[67] which, however, from our perspective, unlike Foucault, we would attribute not to a tendency which is inexorably inscribed in civilization, but to the imbalances dictated by splitting logic triggered by social anguish. In this way, we would appreciate even more the description of the pervasiveness of this power and the elusiveness of its face:

> the multiplicity of force relations immanent in the sphere in which they operate and which constitute their own organization; as the process which, through ceaseless struggles and confrontations, transforms, strengthens, or reverses them; as the support which these force relations find in one another, thus forming a chain or a system, or on the contrary, the disjunctions and contradictions which isolate them from one another; and lastly, as the strategies in which they take effect, whose general design or institutional crystallization is embodied in the state apparatus, in the formulation of the law, in the various social hegemonies.[68]

According to Foucault, psychoanalysis itself is part of power and cannot escape its grip, nor can it claim any kind of immunity from its spells and temptations. However, he writes, relations of power (or power-of-knowledge) involve innumerable points of resistance as their other necessary term. Embedded into the fabric of power relations, these points are usually fully functional for them, *but can also, if necessary, cause radical discontinuities*. I believe that we can, or rather we must, look at psychoanalysis in these terms. Psychoanalysis relies on the power of the word. Now, as Foucault notes, "Discourse transmits and produces power; it reinforces it, but also undermines and exposes it, renders it fragile and makes it possible to thwart it".[69]

Because of the key role it plays in relations between people, sexuality is a sensitive point for the grafting of a discourse of power that is expressed through a form of knowledge. In sexuality, dominated by the arrogance of the desire to know at any cost, abstract logic finds a very fertile ground to take root and grow. On its soil, "the greatest number of maneuvers" and "the most varied strategies"[70] can be developed. Among these, perhaps the main one is the very "production" of the discourse of sexuality, what Foucault calls the "the *deployment of sexuality*",[71] its capacity "in reproducing itself, but in proliferating, innovating, annexing, creating, and penetrating bodies in an increasingly detailed way, and in controlling populations in an increasingly comprehensive way".[72] But for the same reason, because it is highly strategic position, sexuality and the psychoanalytic discourse on sexuality can be an effective point of resistence. It would be difficult to deny this recognition, as, on the other hand, does Foucault himself, who, with respect to psychoanalysis, has oscillated all his life in a kind of perpetual game of *fort/da*, closenes/farness, or love/hate.[73]

However, when psychoanalysis demands a kind of "extra-territoriality" in relation to the State, it is guilty of arrogance, and thus reveals a fragility. At the same time, it asks to be recognized by the very State from which it fears to be normalized.[74] In some of its variants, it claims to authorize itself but then marks its boundaries with a fanaticism that one would expect to find in a sect, not in a community that cultivates scientific and critical thought. It is wary of any reduction to a healthcare "technique",[75] but aspires to be in hospitals and universities (and in general does not disdain frequent power). It does not want to be regulated but gives itself institutions in which there are sometimes exclusionary, opaque, and cruel regulations.

In short, it is difficult for psychoanalysis to be where it should be: not at the very heart of power, but at its margins; if anything, as a point of articulation between inside and outside. Yet it is the only position in which it can represent a critical instance with respect to both power (and to itself as one of its incarnations) and counter-power. Elected to counter-power, but as a critical theory this is not its vocation, it would still be obeying a logic of power—only, reversed in sign. Those who uncritically denounce its inclusion in biopolitics as a technique of normalization, simply turn it into political "chatter". They also demonstrate to be unable to tolerate its essentially aporetic nature.

3.5 Perfect and Invisible

Returning to Freud, his approach to the theme of civilization is congruent with his theory of the etiopathogenesis of neurosis. Freud attributes neurotic suffering to the frustration of sexual life, an explanation that I would not endorse in such direct terms. Rather, today we see every kind of psychological suffering as a manifestation of a cruel internal self-criticism, and thus as an unconscious manifestation of anxiety. The person who suffers psychologically has lost, to varying degrees, that psychoanalytic (but inherently "social") function of the personality that I mentioned earlier. Not only psychosis, but any neurotic symptom can be seen as a sign of a deficit in the ability to make sense of existence; to "dream" emotional experience, so to speak. This conception is not necessarily at odds with Freud's, but it relativizes it and reabsorbs it into a broader vision. It is broader because it looks not only at the individual but at the totality or system of which the individual is a part.

When dealing with the malaise of civilization, reflection almost inevitably follows a binary past/present logic, and there is a tendency to idealize the past and devalue the present. Evil becomes, depending on the case, enlightenment, nihilism, relativism, postmodernism, technology, and science. An authentic historical perspective is missing. In reality, it is not true that things were better when they were worse. Nor should we necessarily adhere to Hegel's optimistic view of the final establishment of the spirit. The problem is different: to diagnose what the new forms of alienation are, without implying that they did not exist yesterday or the day before. They have always been there, though different.

Not even Freud seems to resist the temptation to adopt the same binary code of past/present. But he does so in his own way. When he theorizes that the price of civilization is unhappiness, the term of comparison is merely theoretical. Freud places himself on the level of historicity that includes phylogeny, and therefore more properly on an anthropological level. The analysis of the varying degrees of happiness across different historical epochs is absent from his discourse. To his eyes, civilization, any kind of civilization, no matter at what stage of evolution, implies the repression and suppression of drives. If we consider aggression to be a death drive, what would be the time in human history when destructiveness would not have been expressed?

If it is true that technology has improved the material conditions of life, even if limited to certain populations, and this is still a statistical fact, then in parallel its destructive capacity has also increased. Can we say that one sometimes has the impression that the numbers are about even, or does that sound too outrageous.?[76] The critique of culture therefore makes sense if it does not fall into this easy trap. It is not that Freud himself is completely outside this logic. His contradiction lies in the fact that the object of comparison is no longer a historical epoch, but pre-human animality.

Freud's discourse has the merit of not slipping into the idealization of the more or less immediate historical past. Unlike sociologists, philosophers, or psychoanalysts who, when diagnosing the present, explicitly or implicitly contrast it with the loss of a superior civilization that now belongs to the past, as if we were in a state of decadence, he does not in fact make it a question of epochs. He does not have a naively progressive or regressive vision of History. His is a tragic but penetrating vision precisely because of its absoluteness. Man is this way, period. And always will be. Could one ever say with certainty that an Athenian of the V century B.C. was necessarily more or less happy than a citizen of any metropolis of our days? There have been and continue to be technological innovations and important improvements in the concrete conditions of life of a number of people, but happiness or unhappiness does not depend linearly on this fact.

Moreover, technology produces as many new forms of alienation as it does of emancipation, both material and spiritual. Rather than concluding that if we are not happy, it is because there is some kind of defect at the source, perhaps it would be better to think in dialectical terms about the relationship between culture as the historically determined expression of civilization and civilization as the underlying normative ("transcendental") structure of human existence.

But then, nothing new under the sun? No, certainly not. If not for a linear process of affirmation of man's undivided and mature rationality, on the contrary, in analogy to Kuhn's discourse on scientific paradigms, we can very well think of a succession of more or less balanced cultural paradigms. When a system changes, it is not because the new one trivially "surpasses" it, but because new forms of culture/civilization are produced. What is "new", under the sun, are the unprecedented forms of subjugation that technological innovation produces at an ever-increasing rate and with ever-invasive characteristics with respect to minds and bodies.

In short, it is one thing to think of human society as an entity that inexorably progresses or inexorably regresses (and this is Cassandra-like sociology—like Spengler's) on the basis of some sort of teleological principle, depending on whether it is positive or negative; it is quite another to imagine a complex and multifactorial system that oscillates between moments of greater or lesser stability. By locating happiness in transcendence, religions recognize this essential fact of history's lack of direction. Not so the secularized and absurdly optimistic religions represented by certain political ideologies, which in fact easily produce totalitarian monsters. The "religion of science" is also pernicious in its unattainable arrogance. It discreetly replaces the old metaphysics, cloaks itself in neutrality and objectivity, and is therefore inhuman and dehumanizing.

The point of these notes is to ask, in the wake of what we have said about how psychic suffering is generated in the individual, what the equivalent process might be in the social subject or group. As we have seen, for the individual, the two references to Bion and Winnicott are illuminating in understanding how the split within the ego is first produced. I am alluding to the poignant phenomenon wherein individuals forsake the vital sustenance of their primary needs, most notably the need for genuine recognition and connection, opting instead to barter them for the deplorable currency of abstract rationality and superficial material gratification. In this model, it all starts with the unresponsiveness of the object or environment of care, which can be due to a variety of factors.

The typical situation, as one of my patients described it, is the state of feeling "perfect and invisible". Faced with an unresponsive and unempathetic object, the only way to maintain a fragile bond, that is, to make oneself visible, is to satisfy its demands for perfection. But since this is a conditional visibility, it will in fact always amount to a tragic invisibility. The subject will try harder and harder, but will never be able to feel truly recognized. He will be divided beyond measure. And beyond all measure, it will arrogantly force itself to pursue an anti-human ideal of perfection.

Let us think of the symptom of anorexia/bulimia as the unconscious representation of the dramatic split that occurs early in the primary relationship between the child and the mother, and transpose it onto the body of the social subject. We will better understand Barthes' definition of arrogance as bulimia and of bulimia as a figure of modernity. The girl who has a crisis of bulimia identifies with a mother who forces her to eat because she cannot provide the truth of relational unity as food for the mind.[77] So, on the one hand, she is constantly intruding on her, and on the other hand, she is inducing a state of psychic "hunger". This is the most effective image I know of the split between material life and emotional-spiritual life, of arrogance as an "intrusive" way of relating to oneself and to others. The same girl who exalts herself in anorexic asceticism effectively stages the state of starvation in which she finds herself even when she eats excessively.

But on a collective level, things are no different. Similarly, due to natural or social events, groups find themselves faced with a world for which they have no key, and which is disturbing to them,[78] that is, no longer familiar, but full of anxiety or terror, defensive mechanisms of splitting kick that are entirely analogous to those triggered in the individual. In itself, this is not a bad thing, unless the defenses harden and feed on themselves in a spiral that has no end. What for the individual is the split between psyche and body or between intellect and affection, i.e., the imprisonment in the claustrum of a desiccated way of life, lacking the strength of orientation and integration that emotions have, on the collective level is the ideology of technology or, the triumph of abstraction over thought.[79]

In absolute terms, if we want, nothing new, but in a relative sense every time alienation takes new forms. The problem was already felt in classical antiquity; otherwise, Sophocles would not have enchanted his audience by staging characters who are guilty of arrogance or the same sin of conforming to abstract and absolute logic. Indeed, Oedipus perfectly embodies this technique in his illusory eagerness to know everything. But in Sophocles' time, there were no social networks, no apps, no genetic engineering. There was not the stifling control that for some the 'health terrorism' of our time would impose on people. Updating *Civilization and Its Discontents* today means confronting the task of diagnosing the ever-changing incarnations of technology. What is most striking is the speed with which these innovations reach us and their invasiveness[80] with respect to the body. Even when they increase our cognitive capacities—in fact, we are already talking about augmented reality devices[81]—they simultaneously make us more exposed to forms of control and thus to the reduction of spaces of freedom and ethical life. What is "new" is that every era is called upon to diagnose the unprecedented forms of perversion that technology makes possible and that therefore feed the alienation and cruelty of the social "object".

At the level of the social subject, arrogance mainly takes the form of the idolatry of science and the logic of profit at all costs. According to the Foucauldian idea of power, we cannot imagine that there are potentates dedicated to evil by nature or intention. There are, of course, strong interests represented at various levels. Yet, they are often in conflict with each other and not without deep contradictions within themselves. In short, I do not believe that for a diagnosis of contemporary civilization, it is necessary to identify some agency that is part of society as systematically devoted to perverting the rules of civil life and undermining human happiness. The reason is simple. Assuming that such logics are in place, since they are also unconscious they would themselves fall under the weight of the same basic split that in the individual disconnects abstract logic from bodily intentionality.

I mean that just as in the single individual a false self can take root, as Winnicott describes it with the image of the child who at a certain point withdraws his investment from the object, and thus from himself, or at least greatly limits it, so on the group level a similar defensive mutilation of essential aspects of existence, the same ones that make it worth living, can take place. As in the case of the individual, who unconsciously increases the search for "material" satisfaction because he cannot afford to experience the emotions associated with relationships—he realizes that he would not know where to put them and would come out in pieces—so in the social field the same split takes the form of various and widespread situations of power exercised as a form of domination and alienation.

In both instances, homeostasis is maintained in the short term, but in the long term, the very basis of life is undermined. The psychic ecology of the subject and the psychic ecology of the social subject have the same structure. Both are based on the struggle for recognition. To use Hegel's metaphor, when the "infection" (*Infektion*) is not a contagion that leads to immunization against the disease, as in the case of an effective vaccine, but is a contagion that causes the disease to occur, then people distance themselves from the sociality of the self or from the sociality of others. Fear grows, as does the need for control of bodies and the drive to fill the void of existence with the possession of material goods and perverse forms of life.

Modern technologies now make it possible to realize these control devices in insidious and dangerously intrusive ways.[82] But, I repeat, they should not be seen as an expression of primary, untamable forms of destructiveness—there is no Specter, no Plutocracy or Multinational of Capital or Great Capitalist (or Anti-Capitalist) Conspiracy, etc.; or rather, there are agencies that either seem to play this role or that register genetic mutations in this sense, even on the emotional push of groups in basic assumptions; however, the fact is that they themselves are subject to a logic that is greater than themselves and that they therefore do not control, or only partially control. Around, there is only a tremendous fear. It creates the split that depersonalizes, a fear that dehumanizes. This means that each person is called to take responsibility for his or her own alienation and to construct an ethical life for himself or herself.

For example, if we want to understand what the pure logic of profit corresponds to, we must not reduce it in a moralistic way to greed, pride, and arrogance—which means giving up on understanding—but we must be able to see it as a means of defense against an anxiety that is perceived as overwhelming. The urge to consume, which is undoubtedly a symptom of the condition of contemporary alienation and a fully functional aspect of the logic of profit at all costs, has never been so desperate. From a psychoanalytic perspective, however, even when it takes the form of an obsessive search for emotions, it is nothing more than a desperate attempt to give value to an existence that would otherwise appear dramatically "empty"—the same, however, that we would say of a condemnation of the same behaviors, which would be just as abstract, absolute, and *split*.

When Critical Theory targets the Enlightenment,[83] technology, and the abstract intellect, all of which are not necessarily negative in themselves, it is perfectly correct, but it often fails to offer a convincing vision of why such perversions of civilization occur. Even when it points the way to reconciliation between different instances, it struggles to get out of a vaguely elitist and moralizing atmosphere, like those who "know"; fatally, it becomes arrogant and unempathetic toward what it sometimes identifies as "absolute evil".

In short, instead of helping to heal the split, it sometimes has the effect of deepening and perpetuating it. A typical example, at least in some respects, is Marcuse. An acute critic of the bad present, Marcuse idealizes the aristocratic world that produced the high culture of the Romantic period.[84] He devalues popular culture and all that constitutes material "progress". From his point of view, improving the concrete living conditions of the underprivileged classes would only have the effect of distilling a false consciousness out of unhappiness and sterilise the urge to question the status quo. The world he describes is bleak and paranoid. One can share his diagnosis of some of the logic of alienation in advanced capitalist society, but not the "absolute" tone of the discourse. Marcuse does not seem to realize that such a pessimistic diagnosis, insofar as it is unconditional, is itself a form of *hýbris*.

3.6   A Safe Place

A society for which the antithetical figure of the Achilles/Agamemnon couple (Creon/Antigone, or Bertin/Rameau) is appropriate as a key to interpretation, is a society in which the separation from human emotions implies an extreme emphasis on performance at the cost of dehumanization. On the other hand, a society that dreams of rediscovering a warmer sense of humanity, if it has to be satisfied only with ghosts (as they are for both Achilles and Agamemnon, but also for Creon, all the women—the feminine—with whom they are unable to enter into a truly generative relationship), cannot look to the future.

This may seem like an abstract discourse but it is not. Such a society attacks and sacrifices nature, democracy, life. Of all the tragic figures of arrogance that have accompanied us on our journey, perhaps the one who best sums up our reading of modernity, and of the split that characterizes it, is Achilles. The Greek hero is completely caught up in a negation of himself that cannot be resolved, that is to say, cannot be dialecticized. He would be immortal like a god, but in reality, he is mortal like a man; he is a man, but he has the destructive fury of a god: as Freud[85] says of man, of a "prosthetic God".

Beyond the theoretical and technical solutions that psychoanalysis as therapy has prepared to understand and intervene in the splits of the individual or the small therapy group, it is not easy to say what it can offer on a more general level. To think of pointing to simple solutions, goals, objectives, etc., or to imagine a practice of "liberation" from the ideology of technique would be to presume too much. The exercise of critique, like that of questioning, has in itself its purpose and its what, in its pace and its turning points, but also in its uncertainties and hesitations. To indulge the desire to "solve" the riddle of civilization's malaise, and especially to "cure" it, would be to yield to the same will to power that made Oedipus succumb. As Derrida[86] writes,

> The responsibility for the most just decision must be invented each time in a unique fashion, by each one, in a singular time and space. To hold myself to the letter of our theme, well then, for the "living together" that I am proposing we think beyond any "ensemble," there is no "how", there is, in any case, no "how" that could take the form of precepts, of rules, of norms, or previous criteria available to a knowledge. The "how" must be invented by each at each time. There would be no singular responsibility if a "how" were available in advance to the knowledge of a rule to be applied.

Certainly (and it is in this sense that this contribution is made), as a critical theory, psychoanalysis can first of all contribute to a more precise diagnosis of the malaise of civilization. This is certainly an important first step. Then, but only as suggestions, there remain the examples derived from clinical work. The arrogance of the individual, as we have seen, arises from a basic feeling of fear for the integrity of the self, which leads fatally to a degree of depersonalization. Similarly, the arrogance of society is a form of "sociopathy" or widespread anxiety neurosis that produces similar forms of fragmentation or unreality. As with the individual, what is needed between social subjects of different sizes is the kind of relationality that gives the feeling, inside and out, of being fully entitled to exist.

In order to briefly address in these concluding remarks the issue of what reduces anxiety not only in the individual (actually in the social field concretely constituted by two in the analytic relationship, and on the phantasmatic level by their respective internal groupings), but in the civil community, I would like to reintroduce with another concept of psychoanalysis the essentially analogous, indirect method on which I have based this paper. I refer to the role that the concept of the "safe place" plays in Winnicott's writings, particularly in the third volume of the *Collected Works*. In this volume are collected the essays from 1946 to 1951. It is the period in which it is necessary to heal the wounds of the horrors of war, which Freud seems to have seen coming when he wrote *Civilization and Its Discontents* in 1930. For Winnicott, then, it is a concept in which the confrontation with the unease of civilization is always at the forefront.

The phrase that immediately came to mind when I thought about his essays from this five-year period is "appeal to a safe place". As a great analyst and pediatrician, Winnicott is a writer who is deeply concerned with trauma and distress in relation to society. It is as if he is obsessed with the one thing he considers important. Whether he is talking about antisocial children, about real delinquents, about birth trauma, about hatred in countertransference, the central point is always what is "home" (good environment/primary home experiences/good primary home/child's own home/good start) in which the psyche is born, what endangers the birth, what can be done when the damage has already been done.[87] One must keep in mind the social and historical context that forms the background of these writings. Page after page, the war often appears not only as a memory of recent dramatic experiences but also as a negative figure (broken home/war situation/war time/evacuation breakdown/unsettled homes) of the safe place. This is why, as a possible allegory of the lack of a "safe place", one thinks of Henry Moore's drawings from 1941, exhibited a few years ago at the Tate Gallery, such as *Shelterers in the Tube or Tube Shelter Perspective*, which show Londoners stretched out to sleep in long rows like corpses on the floor of the subway to take shelter from air raids.

A kind of deep conviction animates Winnicott: if he is not too disturbed ("bombed"), the process through which one becomes a mature, integrated subject unfolds naturally. What is needed is to provide support, but without interfering too much with the child's emotional development. Synonyms for "safe place" are stability, continuity, devotion, love, firmness, confidence, "a circle of love and strength (with subsequent tolerance)".[88] The emphasis is on the space that contains and gives form. The adjective "safe" refers more to a way of feeling than to understanding. Rather than "understanding" that one is safe, one "feels" safe.

Essentially there are two main classes of patients, those who have had a fair or good start ("satisfactory consistent personal introduction to the world"[89]), and then have encountered difficulties; and those whose environment, from birth, has failed to fulfill its tasks of providing the nurturing elements that foster the development of the psyche. Where, if not in a "safe place", where one can stay and not be afraid, would one meet the unexpected, fascinating but sometimes disturbing guests that Winnicott presents to us?

For example, the mother (any mother) has no less than seventeen reasons for hating her son; if the child is not touched by hatred, he has no way of believing in the other's love; however much the analyst may love them, he cannot prevent himself from hating his patients; if he shows them love, in the case of serious patients, he must know that he is also "killing" them; to be sentimental about delinquent behavior is harmful because it is unconsciously an expression of hatred; antisocial kids test adults in order to find limits to their impulses and thus not to go crazy—but this is true of every child in general ("business first, the test must be made!"[90])—it is their way of launching an S. O. S: if they don't find someone who is strong but also tolerant and who cares for them, they risk being increasingly unable to express love, they gradually become more depressed and depersonalized no longer able to feel the reality of things; murder also expresses the impulse to grant the victim the pleasure of reliving, in the sensation of suffocation, the contact with the maternal tissues that held him during childbirth; stealing, after all, implies that there remains the hope of encountering something good, outside of this hope there remains only madness and depression.

Winnicott is not afraid to confront Freud and Klein and to express different theses from them. He disagrees with Freud when he seems to think that the mother can only feel love for her child, which also sounds like a subdued but well-deserved claim to originality. Then, when he immediately questions the idea of a normal masochism in women. It is not masochism that is the amazing thing, Winnicott writes, but rather the mother's ability to endure the evil that the child makes her suffer and to hate him so much, but without "paying the child out", renouncing revenge, waiting for expressions of gratitude that may or may not come in a still distant future. How is this possible? And here comes one of those little phrases that leave us admiring and speechless: "Perhaps she is helped by some of the nursery rhymes she sings, which her baby enjoys but fortunately does not understand"? This is followed by a nursery rhyme ("not a sentimental rhyme"), in which a child falls out of the tree: "Rockabye Baby, on the tree top,/When the wind blows the cradle will rock,/When the bough breaks the cradle will fall,/Down will come baby, cradle and all".[91]

It is another example of place/home/*chora semiotics*[92] where one can safely experience hate. With the example of the children's poem, a world opens up about the meaning of play, dream, fiction, art, and the "aesthetic" constitution of the individual. Pain and anger are transformed into something intensely pleasurable. But through what? By the intersubjective creation of a bond, an order, or a structure that operates primarily on the nonverbal or intercorporeal plane. It is curious that for rhymes like these nursery rhymes in Italian, the expression "kissing rhymes" (*rima baciata*) is used to say that it is as if the verses at the end indulge in a sensual contact: in the original text, *top-rock, fall-all*: almost identical but different.

Personal integration is not a given, it is a struggle. Winnicott invites us not to take it for granted that it is easy for people to live in their bodies. It may sound strange that the possibility of being oneself is not guaranteed at birth and that one must conquer it. But that is how it is. Becoming oneself means taking responsibility for one's existence; that involves making sense of even one's most problematic impulses and coming to have enough confidence that one can control them. This is why the care of the "difficult" child in foster homes goes through moments of great turbulence when he or she feels secure enough to try to break out of the shell of a false adaptation. After a period of pseudo-normality, the litmus test comes. The child feels compelled to experience when he can be destructive and how much he can act with impunity. But it may also be the first time he really tries to connect with others. To briefly describe this phase in which, paradoxically, the child begins to hope, Winnicott uses the expression "to get under someone's skin", that is, to make someone nervous or angry, in short, to get inside them[93]—which is the same expression that is sometimes used in analysis to describe those patients whom one takes home, so to speak.

But what happens if a second chance at integration is not given? When the environment continues to fail in its task of meeting the most urgent needs of these suffering people? In dealing with a category of antisocial subjects who are particularly resistant to any treatment, the "habitual offenders",[94] Winnicott comments that they have perfected their criminal technique to the point of deriving pleasure from it, as a violinist from the dexterity of his fingers or a mathematician from his mental agility. The pleasure is in being able to function in a very specialized way and create something beautiful and complex. The comparison is as always both disorienting and illuminating.[95]

In essence, "Winnicott's solution", which I propose here as the paradigm of hospitality to the other, is not based on sentimentality. It would only be another mask of a relationship of domination. Rather, it consists of a certain ability to read and understand the anguish that lies at the origin of the phenomena of pathology (in any case "social") of the individual and society. The "talking cure" of psychoanalysis lies in the experience of love in which mutual recognition essentially consists; an experience for which its own *tékhnē* lays the premises and which it often actually makes possible. These premises are, on the one hand, the provision of a safe material space (an external setting, made up of practical rules); a method of listening (an internal setting) that makes it possible to develop a sense of familiarity, an intimate mutual knowledge; a device of interpretation/finalization (transposed onto the level of society, think of the role of art in general) that, as in the example of the lullaby sung by the mother to the child, does not deny hatred but makes it "singable" (i.e., thinkable), that is, tolerable. Winnicott does not have a naive view of recognition, he does not deny hatred, indeed he says that only when one feels touched by hatred can one also feel touched by love, an idea which in itself is an example of how to reconcile hatred and love, separation and union, intellect, and affectivity.

Notes

1   C. Lasch, *Culture of Narcissism: American Life in an Age of Diminishing Expectations*, (New York: W W Norton & Co., 1991).

2   Z. Bauman, *Liquid Modernity* (2000; Cambridge, UK: Polity Press, 2012).

3   M. Augé, *Non-Lieux. Introduction à une anthropologie de la surmodernité* (1992; Paris: Le Seuil, Paris, 2015).

4   J.-F. Lyotard, *The postmoderncondition*: a report on knowledge, transl. G. Bennington and B. Massumi, (1979; Minneapolis: University of Minnesota Press, 1984).

5   H. Marcuse, *One-Dimensional Man: Studies in the Ideology of Advanced Industrial Society* (1964; London: Routledge, 2002).

6   C. Ternynck, *L'homme de sable: pourquoi l'individualisme nous rend malade* (Paris: Éditions du Seuil, 2011).

7   Cf. S. Freud, *Civilization and Its Discontents*, 88: "the word 'civilization' [*Kultur*] describes the whole sum of the achievements and the regulations which distinguish our lives from those of our animal ancestors and which serve two purposes—namely to protect men against nature and to adjust their mutual relations."

8   R. Barthes, *Barthes by Roland Barthes*, 122.

9   A. H. Pierrot, "Barthes and doxa", *Poetics Today* 23, no. 3 (2002): 427–442, 434.

10 R. Barthes, *Barthes by Roland Barthes*, 153–154.

11 W. R. Bion, *Trasformations* (London: Karnac, 1965).

12 H. Marcuse, *One-Dimensional Man: Studies in the Ideology of Advanced Industrial Society*, xxlvii.

13 Ibid., 3.

14 Cf. Civitarese, W. Minnella, G. Piana, and G. Sandrini, *L'invasione della vita. Le scelte difficili nell'epoca della pandemia* (Udine-Milano: Mimesis, 2020).

15 G. Agamben, *Biosicurezza e politica,* https://www.quodlibet.it/giorgio-agamben-biosicurezza.

16 M. Foucault, *Discipline and Punish: The Birth of the Prison*, transl. A. Sheridan (1975; New York: Vintage Books, 1995).

17 L. Wachowski and A. Wachowski, *The Matrix Revisited* (USA: Australia, 1999).

18 From this point of view, the denunciations of world-renowned intellectuals such as Orhan Pamuk are telling: "The government's pandemic pretext for a stronger grip," *La Repubblica* 27, no. 5 (2021): 15; and F. Fukuyama, "Liberal Democracy has been Under Severe Stress for a Decade, and the Pandemic, Which, Like All Crises, Has Unforeseen Consequences, Further Shrinks the Spaces of Freedom," *Il Corriere della Sera*, 20, no. 5(2021), accessed 23 Feb 2021: https://www.corriere.it/esteri/21_maggio_19/fukuyama-dal-virus-rischi-le-democrazie-molti-leader-vorranno-tenersi-nuovi-poteri-3a95ebbe-b8da-11eb-86a2-256e95d23aef.shtml. UN Secretary-General António Guterres himself, in an speech on *The Guardian* on Thu 25 Feb 2021, (The world faces a pandemic of human rights abuses in the wake of Covid-19), has claimed that "The virus has been used as a pretext in many countries to crush dissent, criminalize freedoms and silence reporting", accessed on 23 May 2021: https://www.theguardian.com/global-development/2021/feb/22/world-faces-pandemic-human-rights-abuses-covid-19-antonio-guterres.

19 Id., *Distanziamento sociale*, https://www.quodlibet.it/giorgio-agamben-distanziamento-sociale.

20 Id., *La medicina come religione,* https://www.quodlibet.it/giorgio-agamben-la-medicina-come-religione.

21 G. Agamben, *A che punto siamo? L'epidemia come politica* (Macerata: Quodlibet, 2020).

22 J. Derrida, "Avowing—The Impossible: 'Returns,' Repentance, and Reconcili-
    ation", [1998]. in *Living Together: Jacques Derrida's Communities of Violence
    and Peace*, ed. E. Weber (New York: Fordham University Press 2013), 18–41,
    79.
23 S. Freud, *Civilization and its Discontents*, (1930), 68.
24 Ibid., 66.
25 Ibid., 122. Elsewhere, Freud writes that Eros has the task "by bringing about a
    more and more far-reaching combination of the particles into which living sub-
    stance is dispersed, aims at complicating life and at the same time, of course,
    at preserving it" (S. Freud, "The Ego and the Id," *The Standard Edition of the
    Complete Psychological Works of Sigmund Freud* 19, (1923): 1–66, 40). Libido
    then, as a partial expression of it, evolved and closer to experience, falls under
    Eros, which is the much broader, yet also more speculative concept by which
    from 1920 onwards Freud denotes the set of life drives (*Lebenstriebe*) as op-
    posed to death drives. If libido implies the human dimension of desire, Eros
    accounts for a drive that may originally be merely biological or somatic.
26 Cf. M. Heidegger, *The Fundamental Concepts of Metaphysics: World, Fini-
    tude, Solitude*, transl. W. McNeill and N. Walker (1983; Bloomington, IN: In-
    diana Univ Press, 2001), 176: "the animal is poor in world [*weltarm*]". See also
    G. Agamben, "Poverty in world", in *Id., The Open: Man and Animal*, transl. K.
    Attell (2002; Stanford, CA: Stanford University Press, 2004).
27 S. Freud, *Civilization and its Discontents*, (1930), 120.
28 Ibid., 121.
29 Ibid.
30 Ibid., 128.
31 Ibid., 123–124.
32 R. Mancini, *Le logiche del male. Teoria critica e rinascita della società*, 83,
    italics added.
33 E. Fromm, *The anatomy of human destructiveness* (1973; New York: Henry
    Holt & Co, 1992).
34 M. Foucault, *Lectures on the Will to Know and Oedipal Knowledge: Lectures
    at the Collège de France 1970–1971*, transl. G. Burchell (London: Palgrave
    Macmillan, 2013), 196.
35 S. Freud, *Civilization and Its Discontents*, (1930), 111.
36 Ibid., 124.
37 Ibid., 130, fn.
38 Ibid., 124.
39 Ibid., 128.
40 Ibid., 130.
41 Ibid., 133.
42 Cf. di Battista, *La fine dell'innocenza. Utopia, totalitarismo e comunismo*
    (Venezia: Marsilio, 2000).
43 S. Freud, *Civilization and its Discontents*, (1930), 104.
44 Ibid., 104.

45 Ibid., 112.
46 Ibid., 105.
47 M. Foucault, *History of sexuality, vol.1: An Introduction*, transl. R. Hurley (1976; New York: Pantheon Books, 1978), Ibid., 32.
48 Ibid., 17.
49 H. Marcuse, *One-Dimensional Man: Studies in the Ideology of Advanced Industrial Society*, 59.
50 Ibid., 7
51 Ibid., 76–77.
52 Ibid., 80
53 Ibid., 89.
54 Ibid., 98–100.
55 M. Foucault, *The History of Sexuality. Volume I: An Introduction*, 37.
56 Ibid., 40.
57 Ibid., 48.
58 Ibid., 49
59 Ibid., 53.
60 Ibid., 55.
61 Ibid., 67. Foreign to the Kafkaesque world described by Foucault is the Hegelian conception of confession as a means, along with forgiveness, of achieving genuine intersubjective recognition. On this, see F. Falappa, *Il cuore della ragione. Dialettiche dell'amore e del perdono in Hegel*.
62 Ibid., 68.
63 Ibid., 73.
64 Ibid., 77
65 Ibid., 78.
66 Ibid., 81.
67 Ibid., 93.
68 Ibid., 92–93.
69 Ibid., 101.
70 Ibid., 103.
71 Ibid., 106.
72 Ibid., 107.
73 Cf. J. Derrida, "'To Do Justice to Freud': The History of Madness in the Age of Psychoanalysis," Transl. A. Brault and M. Naas, *Critical Inquiry* 20, no. 2 (Winter, 1994): 227–266: "Would Foucault's project have been possible without psychoanalysis, with which it is contemporary and of which it speaks little and in such an equivocal or ambivalent manner in the book?" (233). And further: "Psychoanalysis, on the contrary, breaks with psychology *by speaking with the Unreason* that speaks within madness and, thus, by returning through this exchange of words not to the classical age itself-which also determined madness as unreason, but, unlike psychology, did so only in order to exclude or confine it-but toward this eve of the classical age that still haunted it." (237–238). The fact is, he seems to conclude, that "The

contradiction is no doubt in the things themselves, so to speak. [...] This does not mean, however, that we, without ever finding him to be radically wrong or at fault, have to subscribe a priori to all his statements" (251). A concept that he effectively reiterates later: "only those who work, only those who take risks in working, encounter difficulties. One only ever thinks and takes responsibility—if indeed one ever does—in the testing of the aporia; without this, one is content to follow an inclination or apply a program" (262–263). Indeed, Foucault has always been ambivalent about psychoanalysis. For example, see M. Foucault, *Mental Illness and Psychology* [1954], transl. A. Sheridan (1954; Berkeley & Los Angeles: University of California Press, 1987) 80: "madness, which had for so long be overt and unrestricted, which had for so long be present on the horizon, disappeared. It entered a phase of silence from which it was not to emerge for a long time; it was deprived of its language; and although one continued to speak of it, it became impossible for it to speak of itself. *Impossible at least until Freud, who was the first to open up once again* the possibility for reason and unreason to communicate in the danger of a common language, ever ready to break down or disintegrate into the inaccessible" (69); and also, in *The History of Sexuality. Volume I: An Introduction*, 133, italics added: "It is to the political credit of psychoanalysis-or at least, of what was most coherent in it-that it regarded with suspicion (and this from its inception, that is, from the moment it broke away from the neuropsychiatry of degenerescence) the irrevocably proliferating aspects which might be contained in these power mechanisms aimed at controlling and administering the everyday life of sexuality [...] *It was owing to this that psychoanalysis was—in the main, with a few exceptions—in theoretical and practical opposition to fascism.* On the relation between Foucault and Freud, see also J. Whitebook, "Against Interiority: Foucault's Struggle with Psychoanalysis", in *The Cambridge Companion to Foucault*, ed. G. Gutting (Cambridge: Cambridge University Press, 2005), 312–347.

74 In this regard, it is instructive to read the manifesto of the "General States of Psychoanalysis", in J. Derrida, "Psychoanalysis Searches the States of Its Soul: The Impossible Beyond of Sovereign Cruelty", *Without Alibi*, transl. Kamuf (2000; Stanford, CA: Stanford University Press, 2002), 238–280.

75 Cf. Ricoeur, "Technique and Nontechnique in Interpretation," in *The Conflict of Interpretations: Essays in Hermeneutics,* transl. W. Domingo (1969; Evanston, IL: Northwestern University Press, Evanston, IL, 1974), 177–195, https://books.google.it/books?id=0QuXVWzxoLIC&printsec=frontcover&hl=it#v=onepage&q=heath%20&f=false

76 J. Derrida, "Avowing—The Impossible: 'Returns,' Repentance, and Reconciliation," in *Living Together: Jacques Derrida's Communities of Violence and Peace*, ed. E. Weber (1998), 38: "For the eloquent and meticulous militants of the rights of men and of social struggles in their countries should never forget that never, in the entire history of humanity, have so many people on earth been lacking bread and drinkable water".

77 Cf. W. R. Bion, *Trasformations,* (1965; London: Karnac, 1991), 38: "healthy mental growth seems to depend on truth as the living organism depends on food. If it is lacking or deficient the personality deteriorates."

78 Cf. A. Moroni, *Sul perturbante. Attualità e trasformazioni di un'idea freudiana nella società e nella clinica psicoanalitica di oggi* (Udine-Milano, 2019).

79 Cf. R. Mancini, *La fragilità dello spirito. Leggere Hegel per comprendere il mondo globale.*

80 Cf. G. Civitarese, "Do Cyborgs Dream? Post-Human Landscapes in Shinya Tsukamoto's in *Nightmare Detective,*" *The International Journal of Psycho-Analysis* 91, no. 4 (2006): 1005–1016, 2010.

81 In his latest novel, *Klara and the Sun* (Alfred A. Knopf: New York, 2021), Kazuo Ishiguro imagines a future in which access to higher-education is effectively barred to students who do not have "enhanced" DNA.

82 Apple has informed the press that it is programming an algorithm to search for child pornography in all the photos stored in iCloud by iPhone users in the United States. Of course, nobody would dare to question the sense of such an initiative, except that: a) it doesn't come from a government agency, but from a private company, whose levels of public accountability and structure of decision-making processes are obviously different; b) we realize our total subservience to technology the moment it becomes possible for someone to penetrate our most intimate sphere of life, in this case, I repeat, with good intentions... but don't they say that good intentions pave the way to hell? Curiously, we also recently learned of the breach, followed by a ransom demand, of the database containing all the health data of the Lazio region, and of the malware installed on the mobile phones of prime ministers of various nations in order to spy on them. On the concept of 'invasive object' in psychoanalysis, however, see, by Williams, *Invasive Objects Minds Under Siege* (London: Routledge, 2010).

83 Cf. M. Horkheimer and T. W. Adorno, *Dialectic of Enlightenment: Philosophical Fragments*, transl. E. Jephcott, (1947; Stanford, CA: Stanford University Press, 2002), 66: "Enlightenment, however, is the philosophy which equates truth with the scientific system".

84 H. Marcuse, *One-Dimensional Man: Studies in the Ideology of Advanced Industrial Society*, 62–63: "Surely, the world of their predecessors was a backward, pre-technological world, a world with the good conscience of inequality and toil, in which labor was still a fated misfortune; but a world in which man and nature were not yet organized as things and instrumentalities. With its code of forms and manners, with the style and vocabulary of its literature and philosophy, this past culture expressed the rhythm and content of a universe in which valleys and forests, villages and inns, nobles and villains, salons and courts were a part of the experienced reality. In the verse and prose of this pre-technological culture is the rhythm of those who wander or ride in carriages, who have the time and the pleasure to think, contemplate, feel and narrate."

85 S. Freud, *Civilization and its Discontents*, (1930), 91–92: "by his science and technology [...] Man has, as it were, become a kind of prosthetic God. When

he puts on all his auxiliary organs he is truly magnificent; but those organs have not grown on to him and they still give him much trouble at times". The "new and probably unimaginably great advances in this field of civilization [...] will increase man's likeness to God still more", Freud (ibid.) writes. The prediction is coming true: newspapers have reported that the Neuralink chip, the hardware designed by Elonk Musk to be implanted in the brain in order to improve its performance, is ready.

86 J. Derrida, "Avowing—The Impossible: 'Returns,' Repentance, and Reconciliation," in *Living Together: Jacques Derrida's Communities of Violence and Peace.*, ed. E. Weber, 18–41, 34.

87 On the concept of home, cf. G. Civitarese and S. Boffito, "Intime stanze. La casa della psicoanalisi", in AAVV., *Le case dell'uomo. Abitare il mondo*, 29–42, Utet, Torino, 2016. See also S. Petrosino, *Lo spirito della casa. Ospitalità, intimità e giustizia*, 46–47: "In walking through that room, in opening that window, in re-dressing that bed and that kitchen, the subject is invested with memories, sensations, feelings, and so, without having properly decided to do so, he finds himself revising, reliving and rethinking, imagining and fantasizing, as if he is taken in by a stream of emotions and words that reveals to him how that room and that window, that bed and that kitchen were never mere objects at his disposal or mere spaces to be occupied, being rather his own place, 'his own home' without property." Lastly, cf. J. Derrida, *Adieu to Emmanuel Levinas*, transl. A. Brault and M. Naas (1997; Standford, CA: Stanford University Press, 1999), 41–42: "the one who welcomes the invited or received *hôte* (the guest), the welcomimg *hôte* who considwers himself the owner of the place, is in truth a *hôte* received in his own home. He receives the hospitality that he offers in his own home [...] The one who invites is invited by the one whom he invites".

88 D. W. Winnicott, *The Collected Works of D.W. Winnicott, Volume 3, 1946-1951*, (Oxford: Oxford University Press, 2017), 45.

89 Ibid., 33.

90 Ibid., 45.

91 Ibid., 67.

92 Cf. J. Kristeva,. *Revolution in Poetic Language*, transl. M. Waller (1974; New York: Columbia University Press, 1984).

93 D. W. Winnicott, *The Collected Works of D.W. Winnicott, Volume 3, 1946-1951*, 92.

94 Ibid., 53.

95 Ibid., 316.

Chapter 4

Recognition

4.1 Confession/forgiveness

The safe place, as we have just seen, is the inner sense of being able to trust oneself and others sufficiently. It is the basic trust (faith) that is earned in interpersonal relationships; more specifically, it is structured from the bonds that are woven with the other each time the spark of recognition is ignited. Effective recognition must be mutual. In the moment in which it occurs, it can only be based on a relationship that is not asymmetrical but one of equality. As Pinkard[1] writes, "Benevolence or love does not involve the submergence of my personality".

In its molecular structure, Hegel teaches that the dynamics of recognition obeys the logic of confession and forgiveness, not to be understood, of course, in the sense that these concepts have in the Catholic religion, but as allegorical terms of the fine dialectical movement that underlies the I-other identification. What each person "confesses" is the desire for the desire of the Other,[2] that is to say, trivially, to love and to be loved in return, and at the same time the sin (with attached sense of guilt) of the in-difference (that is, the difference or asymmetry that are characteristic of unequal relationships) that he *previously* felt towards the other. At the same time, confession is also about *irreducible* difference, i.e., the awareness that such a desire is destined never to be entirely satisfied,[3] the impossibility of it being exclusive and total.[4] Every confession, then, implies a request for forgiveness and confession on the part of the other. In confession, the individual externalizes something internal, takes it out of himself and, so to speak, hands it over (alienates) to the will of the other. Forgiveness is the reverse movement whereby something internal is removed and replaced by something that is received from the other.

The path of recognition could not but pass through the awareness, shared with the other, that I can only be myself if the other recognizes me, that is, if

DOI: 10.4324/9781032669427-5

I come to live in her/him as a part of her/him, and through the reciprocation of the same confession, which we can also call "forgiveness". In essence, in recognition, confession and forgiveness imply each other, they are inseparable. Similarly, not even repentance as a painful awareness of difference (reducible and irreducible) can be dissociated from confession, indeed it is its presupposition.

The basic "difference", inescapable and irreducible, which we must confess and which must be confessed to us, which we must forgive and which we must be forgiven for, at its lowest level coincides with the very fact of living (and indeed, in writing, for a kind of modesty we say "we" instead of "I"), with subjectivity as a necessary but not sufficient element (intersubjectivity is also needed) for the constitution of the human subject. We might define it as the *hýbris* inherent in the mere act of existing as self-assertion. This difference, from the physiological and functional, can become extreme, for example, when it takes the form of a relationship of exploitation and violence.

We will then have situations in which we speak of confession, repentance, and forgiveness as concrete acts; in which we witness, for example, the mediatized spectacle of requests for forgiveness and repentance[5] addressed to victims and perpetrators of serious crimes. Such pleas can easily sound as hypocritical. However, the "unconscious" logic behind them also escapes the false consciousness of those who invoke them as a way, only apparently blunt and instrumental, of resolving the conflict that lacerates the conscience of society. In fact, there is a deep collective need to reintegrate the outsider. The group needs to heal the scandalous rift within itself as soon as possible. In essence, then, we are not dealing with different cases, but with different dimensional scales. At the various levels at which it can manifest itself—metapsychological, existential, therapeutic, and media—the dynamic of confession-forgiveness (with Klein, we would say: guilt-reparation) is the invariant of the structure of recognition.[6]

The relationship of mutual implication that exists between confession and forgiveness is what we call "reciprocity". One is born psychically only through mutual mediation. At this point, love and truth, singularity and universality, subject and community coincide. In the subject, the recognition of the other is also the means for the recognition of the many others (the Other/the "divine" universality of language) that inhabit it and vice versa.

It goes without saying that when reciprocity is lacking, problems arise. If, from our point of view, confession, any confession, is a declaration (as in "declaring" your love to someone), a clarification of what is obscure, it is nevertheless never a risk-free declaration. The risk is precisely the lack of reciprocity. But, again, a certain lack of reciprocity is also necessary. In a situation of total fusion (symbiosis, gregarious community; exclusive membership, and therefore excluding), the very possibility of the dialectical binomial "confession-forgiveness" would come to nothing.

Understood in this way, both confession and forgiveness are not only "inseparable" but also "impossible", in the sense that they cannot be "decided" but only allowed to happen. They can also consist of intentional acts, but they involve the sphere of affectivity (which guarantees their non-falseness), and therefore cannot be predetermined. Since conscious recognition alone cannot guarantee this relationship of equality, only the logic of *Liebe* can do so; only this logic can be attributed to the power to heal the wound of non-recognition. We should then go beyond a clear distinction between interiority and exteriority, because the former one continually curves into the latter and vice versa. If the subject does not have faith in the possibility of being reciprocated by the internal object, then he is incapable of concrete acts of declaration-confession and declaration-forgiveness (of difference) toward the other.

Conscious and voluntary recognition, which is of obvious importance, all the more so when it is less ambiguous or conflictual, could still conceal an intimate split between intellect and reason, if by "reason" we mean a function of ideo-affective integration that expresses the subject's non-split intentionality.

In analysis, one way in which conscious and voluntary recognition is carried out consists in the practice of listening to the sense of unconscious communication, not in terms of the separation of the *I/you*, but in terms of the reconciliation expressed by the *we*. If there is a curiosity to know the other, if this drive to individuate oneself in infinity is not inhibited, then it may be that the emotional-affective knowledge that lies at the heart of the bond is consonant with representational knowledge. At the bottom of the "cure", of whatever presents itself as technique and knowledge, there is always the possibility of mutual recognition based on the logic of *love*, and within which lives the spectrality of the pairs of guilt-repentance and confession-forgiveness.

Foucault does not seem to recognize this dimension in psychoanalysis (or only with a certain ambivalence), which for us instead is the most essential one, and superficially assimilates the technique of free association to religious or judicial confession. But these particular cases would only represent a perversion, which is certainly possible, of a process that ideally and practically has an entirely different meaning. To tell the truth, on a speculative rather than practical level, we could paradoxically see the *same* meaning. It would make sense from a certain point of view, but we would be making a bundle out of all the herbs: Romeo's confession of love to Juliet would be no different from an *auto-da-fé*.

In the confession-forgiveness, we can see that there is an assumption of responsibility for identity and difference. If we think of situations in which a community that feels marginalized asks to be recognized, but at the same time closes itself in a position of absolutism of difference, which itself becomes a source of violence, we realize how easily we can tend to erase one of the two terms of the dialectical relationship between identity and difference. In this way, we avoid taking responsibility for them, which requires work and tolerance of the frustration that comes from being essentially uncompleted subjects.[7]

Not even in the therapeutic relationship can there be confession and forgiveness without mutuality. It would be a one-sided act.[8] It would not bring about unison, the state of emotional communion from which alone the truth that nourishes the mind can derive. Just as a dream becomes such only upon awakening, so love only becomes such when it is reciprocated. Unrequited love, on either side, remains sterile; in fact, it is "logically" impossible. At best, it is an unhappy love, but it is not love, not even in those who feel it; if anything, it is failure. Not for nothing does it often turn into hate, as we see paradigmatically in the erotomanic delirium. A similar concept can be found in perhaps the most famous verse of the *Inferno*[9] which reads "Amor, ch'a nullo amato amar perdona [Love, that exempts no one beloved from loving]". No one who is loved can be "forgiven" for not loving; but if he cannot not love in return, neither is he spared the Freudian "fear of the loss of love [*Angst vor dem Liebesverlust*]".[10]

Of course, such a situation can occur, but then it would be something else, obsession, perversion, psychosis, unhappiness. And unhappiness can be said to be forgiveness without the repentance of the forgiven, which, when present, is equivalent to his own confession-forgiveness. At the same time, eschewing the arrogance of will and conscience, one might think that any act of forgiveness can only be unilateral, in the sense of not depending on any conditionality, on "no calculation, whether sublime or spiritual",[11] *but could it ever be "unilateral" on the phantasmatic plane?*

An inevitable moment in the process of recognition is also the aspect of fatigue and "struggle". In fact, the conflictual element corresponds to the awareness of the *difference* between the subject and the other. The difference is the friction that they must overcome in order to become one. It automatically creates a competition for the predominance of the point of view of one or the other, which in itself generates tension, anxiety, or pain; but then, like a spring that compressed tends to generate an opposite movement, it also pushes towards reconciliation. Soon, both agents realize that, at least for what is really important, since it concerns the feeling of existing, the partial point of view of each has no value until it is validated by the other, and that if each remains in its own absolute ("arrogant") position, separation and unhappiness could increase and lead to the end of the relationship.

Although the struggle for recognition that is inherent in every human interaction, even the most innocuous and trivial, may unfold violently, it does not seem to be so at all. In fact, it usually goes completely unnoticed. It would be better defined as "work". In fact, it is the so-called work of the negative. Just as we breathe, we are always engaged, both biologically and spiritually, in reducing (denying) differences, that is, in overcoming the cleavages of reality and thus gaining a sense of identity. In order to be authentic, I repeat, and although a certain ambivalence is inevitable, as in life, in the analytical setting recognition cannot be limited to the aspect of the will or be merely cognitive (conscious and unconscious). Rather, it must also take place on the level of feeling (conscious and unconscious).

The fact is that you cannot force yourself to love. To avoid falling into a position of antithetical opposition, we will have to admit that there may be various levels, arranged along a continuum, of recognition. Just as there are many kinds of people, Tolstoy makes Anna Karenina say, so there are many kinds of love. In some cases, a simple formal validation may be sufficient. For others, it may be that only love understood in the romantic sense, of which Freudian transference love is only a variant, will suffice.[12]

Especially in the latter case, where the most intimate sense of a person's existence is at stake, the precondition for an effective, real reconciliation is that a relationship of equals is established. In practice, both in analysis and in daily life, scientific curiosity, even abstract interest, frequentation, familiarity, availability, intellectual understanding, are useful. These are all factors that can contribute indirectly to laying the groundwork for recognition, but they are not sufficient if the change is to affect deep areas of the personality. On the contrary, if, dictated by an abstract demand for knowledge at any cost, the principle of having-to-be were in force, this would be fatally at odds with the hospitality for the other that lies at the heart of the logic of *Liebe*. Such a situation would have the sense not of healing but of re-proposing the split. Indeed, having-to-be always implies a reservation about the being that peers ahead. It is true, as Kojève[13] says, that recognition is "a knowing action [*action connaissante, une connaissance active*]", but this does not in any way guarantee that there is no division between what is more properly a knowledge based on the intellect and knowledge that also involves affectivity.

In analysis, the theories and the corresponding technical devices that promote the overcoming of the *I/you* split and the rediscovery of the "we" develop more effective antibodies to counteract the asymmetry, which is dialectically necessary, of the relationship. Overcoming the *I/you* split (the sphere of mere relationship) is not possible unless we also overcome the split between abstract rationality (intellect) and the erotic/affective body (sensibility). Finally, reconciliation should not be seen as an event that happens once and for all. Ideally, it is *always* happening or *not* happening. The subject's feeling of vitality needs to be continually nurtured. It coincides with coming to be a subject, a lifelong process. It could be described as becoming both more *finite* (individuated, with a strengthened ego) and *infinite* (with a larger and more tolerant soul, with more perspectives on things, richer in humanity). If things go well, that is, if he is not confronted with an excess of "difference" (in a more concrete sense, with an amount of traumatic stimuli), the individual reaches a balance, and never a situation of absolute fusion with the other. Such an eventuality, as we have seen, would not even be desirable. It would be tantamount to completely zeroing out the difference and therefore one of the two necessary poles of the dialectic of subjectivation.

But let us now re-describe the same dynamic starting from the key concept that in Bion accounts for the therapeutic action, the at-one-ment, the moments of "being one" of analyst and patient.

4.2 At-one-ment

If we consider that for Bion the at-one-ment corresponds to the intersubjective *truth* that is generated between mother and child (or between any two individuals) when a situation of emotional attunement takes place, and that as such it is the food that allows psychic growth, the best definition we have, in my opinion, is to be found once again, in Hegel[14]: "the living substance is the being that is in truth *subject*, [...] is only this *self-restoring* sameness, the reflective turn into itself in its otherness.—The true is not an *original unity* as such, or, not an *immediate* unity as such. It is the coming-to-be of itself, the circle that presupposes its end as its goal and has its end for its beginning, and which is actual only through this accomplishment and its end".

The central idea seems to me to be that truth is no longer a static concept (content) but a *process*, a becoming, a living in a dimension that is *trans-individual*. Being at one with the other (in unison) is a state that is inevitably lost and regained each time, since it coincides in this same movement, *nor could it be otherwise*, whereby one sees himself reflected by the other, and therefore, if he recognizes himself, he sees himself both as the self that was and as the self that has meanwhile become (and therefore different), and reciprocally. Their mutual recognition, the *feeling* that corresponds to it, constitutes their *truth*.

In this "truth", which coincides with the common essence, there is nothing fixed or prefixed, nothing absolutely conscious/active or absolutely unconscious/passive. This process, then, that we could define as becoming oneself or becoming a subject, could never only concern the dyad self-other, but always also that self-Other, where with a capital letter we indicate the sociality that participates in it through the forms of intersubjectivity, both pre-reflective or instinctual and reflexive or linguistic. From the polarity of intersubjectivity, which together with that of subjectivity "constitutes" the subject, the individual's becoming a subject and the group's becoming a social subject (or community) proceed simultaneously.

At-one-ment or 'truth' or 'value' or 'bond' is then nothing but the happy outcome of an interpersonal negotiation that takes place consciously, but mostly unconsciously. In fact, Antigone declares that she does not know where the (eternal) laws that drive her to act as she does come from—the norms of the social space in which she lives, which is therefore to be understood as an "ethical" space, that is, a space in which in discourse each person is constantly engaged in giving reasons for his or her actions and in assuming obligations.[15] The negotiation of one's own status as a person is unconscious in a twofold sense: first, because it is partly unconscious, and second, because *it also involves intercorporeality (emotions, feelings, patterns of action)*, that is, an area that cannot be expressed verbally. We can therefore say that it consists of a *form* of living, which is ultimately a "second nature".[16]

In the dialectic of intersubjective recognition, what is at stake is the *value* of each person's self as reflected in the eyes of the other. If I confess to myself that I am sensitive to the value that the other ascribes to me, I make myself vulnerable to the mortification of discovering that I may have none for him. Like Bertin, I would see the abyss of abjection open wide before me. At the same time, if I am interested in the value that the other ascribes to me, it is because I ascribe it to her/him, otherwise I would be completely indifferent to what she/he thinks. The risk of mortification forces me to realize that we are on an *equal* footing. Consequently, I can differentiate myself as a subject only if I do not appear *indifferent* to the other, only if I appear "different" to him, that is, not as a thing among things, and vice versa the other to me. The value that I have for the other and that the other has for me constitutes *our* truth and at the same time *my* truth. What is true for me can only be true if it is also true for the other. Something has the value of truth when it is of the order of being common to both of us when neither of us is uninterested in it.

The true meaning of analytic care is to initiate a process that over time makes one less and less *in*different to the other; said otherwise, that leads to the constitution of a baggage of shared truths, or to a mutual feeling of worth in the eyes of the other. "Value", "truth", "bond" are thus the terms that give an account of the degree of falsity or authenticity of the self or of *freedom*, understood as freedom from a relationship of mere domination-indifference; Bion would say: freedom from a relationship under the banner of mere intellectual knowledge of the other (in minus-K; where K stands for "knowledge") and not under the banner of experience (in O)—since K (without the minus sign in front) is to be reserved for curiosity that may eventually lead to O.[17]

For his family, Ivan Ilyich died long before he died, because they don't care much about him. Even if he is still alive, Ivan Ilyich has already ceased to exist. If I am not affectively (emotion=measure of value) attached to someone who recognizes me, I don't know what to do with it. Recognition remains purely intellectual, abstract, and instrumental. It is the situation of one who is loved but does not love in return. In the treatment, sensing what the unconscious emotional experience shared by the patient and the analyst is at any given moment means to be concerned about how much this can correspond to *hatred*, that is, the opposite of *truth-linking-value-freedom*. It is hatred that Bion saw in arrogance in his psychotic patients as an element of the symptomatological triad of curiosity, arrogance, and stupidity.

At-one-ment corresponds to the creation of a third, "objective", "universal", impersonal point of view, which takes each of the individual subjects out of their absolute point of view and thus allows them to resolve the conflict between the different points of view. The *social* construction of this third point of view (which is also a point of "feeling"), truth, table of values, is what we call the process of subjectivation. The "difference" lies in the difference of points of view. Settling the difference means entering into a relationship in which each person describes and redescribes the other from his or her own point of view, including aspects that are alien to him or her, until some form of reconciliation is achieved.

It is the activity of *coordination*. The link is the union of two different points of view to form a common point of view, to realize an intimate tuning. Each link realizes the difference of the common point of view on what is true, authoritative, worthy, compared to all subjective points of view. It is worth noting again that the common point of view is first of all a sensitive concept, which then may also acquires proper intellectual or abstract content. Unity concerns both cognitive (concepts) and evaluative (emotions) points of view. In fact, emotion is an "affective" view of things and, as such, never ceases to express an evaluation of them.

The "subjectivity" of the subject, Pinkard writes, "What counts as the 'individuality' of the individual is not something that is the 'real thing' (the *Sache selbsts*) that transcends contingency or circumstance; it is as much a part of the pattern of social recognition as its expression were taken to be".[18] The description of the way in which this recognition can take place, i.e. the mutual access between "individuals" requires postulating a pre-existing and transcendental community, a preliminary state of co-belonging—and thus a condition of *sameness*, albeit partial, corresponding to it—with regard to the experience that each has of himself as an agent distinct from the others. The individuality (*distinctiveness, uniqueness, singularity*) of the individual, i.e., the set of qualities that make him *other* than the other, could not be achieved without a form of "continuity" or "co-extensiveness" or "sameness" *always already given* between them. In the individual (or subject), the relationship between individuality and identicality is dialectical, since each term is denied but also preserved by the other as a necessary precondition for its own definition.

"The *I* that is *we* and the *we* that is *I*"[19] cannot be thought of as the mere sum of several *I*'s connected by a bond of relationality, but rather as the unity (as well as in a group) in which the individual *I*'s lose at least in part their distinctiveness, a "whole", a singular entity or organism placed in space and time, not as a single self. It would not be enough to say that singularities are defined by the positions they assume in social space; they are also defined by the positions they assume in the social space that is established in the interiority of each person and that therefore also represents an area of overlap or indistinction (properly intersubjective or transindividual). From the *I/you* of mere difference, it would therefore be necessary to rediscover the *I(you)-you(I)*, the chiasmatic structure of identity, that is, to rediscover the "we" of the linking.

One feels "at home", that is, fulfilled when one lives in accordance with the ethicality of the social space. Hegel[20] writes: "The reconciling *yes*, in which both I's let go of their opposed *existence*, is the existence of the *I* extended into two-ness [*If I discover that I have something in common with another, my Ego expands and not the other way round. It may be a trivial piece of information or a passion we share, but the mechanism is identical*], which therein remains the same as itself and which has the certainty of itself in its complete self-relinquishing and in its opposite.—It is the God who appears in the midst of those who know themselves as pure knowing". Obviously, Pinkard[21] explains, "God" is not the transcendent and metaphysical God, but "what is divinely immanent within human life itself as the human community has come to understand itself. What we take as sacred—[…] What we consider *sacred*—the divine—are the things that for us have come to have absolute value".

Again, at-one-ment comes from *atonement*, which means expiation, reconciliation, and redemption. It is an act of reparation; even if, unlike Bion, Melanie Klein, to whom we owe this concept, does not theorize its reciprocity, i.e., paradoxically, it is also the mother who must "repair" the damage done to the child in the unconscious phantasy (and by analogy the analyst to the patient, or any subject to an object with whom he has a bond). At-one-ment has to do with righting a wrong by confessing guilt and obtaining forgiveness. The wrong is always done both to the other as an individual and to God, where "God" is the name we give to the infinite and symmetrical dimension of the community and therefore also to the intersubjective pole of the subject.

At the root of any wrong is then always the arrogance of considering oneself different (superior) to the other. In other words, it is *difference* pure and simple; the original sin of the very fact of existing, that is, of *ek-sistere* in the double meaning of "coming out of oneself" appropriating the other and at the same time coming out of a state of primordial indifferentiation. As we see most glaringly in Sophocles, the condition of existing is inherently tragic, and wrongness emanates from something that, already in its mode of being alone, the subject *had to do* or *could not avoid doing*. Otherwise, tragedy and life (*any* life) would not be inherently noble. "Tragedy" is, from a certain point of view, the Ego (according to Valéry, "The proudest of the stars"!) is both "obliged" and legitimated to be, to differentiate itself, that which truly represents the *zero degree of arrogance*.[22] But in doing so, the individual subject inevitably distances himself from the "God" of his communitarian substance, or rather from the "social divine"[23] that is essential to the harmony of life. Sin is thus always a sin of *hýbris*, and yet a *necessary* one.

In normal social practices, the individual is constantly required to "suppress" himself as such in order to adopt the community's point of view. At the same time, the more he identifies with everyone's values, the more he is validated and the more he asserts himself as an individual, this time by "suppressing" the impersonal *one-has-to* of the community. Self-awareness is a "self-image" (the "story" of the self), and the description/image one gives of oneself expresses what values are at stake in being oneself. Each person thinks of himself (self-understands/"tells" himself) as a particular "type", i.e., as a person who typically does certain things and in this way differs from other types, or better still, as an "individual" who differs from the mass of other individuals and whose uniqueness does not fit into any *pre-given* type. The ego itself is "empty", it is only "pure consciousness". It can only find itself or its identity outside itself, in what others think it is. This is why we say that the ego is constitutively *alienated* or *foreign*.

However, there is a big difference between the physiological and constitutive alienation of the ego and the alienation that generates anguish and disease. In the second case what is corrupted is the dialectical game between subjectivity and intersubjectivity. This happens when, driven by anxiety, one of the two terms takes dominance over the other. It is then that arrogance-*hýbris* is triggered. Having a heightened sensitivity to these phenomena when they do not yet present themselves as *overtly* pathological, we can believe that it helps to diagnose the split in both individual and collective forms of unhappiness.

By showing the results of a double blindness, Sophocles as the author of *Antigone* and Hegel (just as brilliantly) with his critical reading shows us what is at the basis of ethical life: not a principle of absolutism but a principle of hospitality. The first presents it as a balance between the individual and the community (between οἶκος and *pòlis*). The second shows us that this balance is achieved through the logic of recognition, the fine structure of which, as we have seen, corresponds to the reconciliatory dynamics of confession and forgiveness. The same dialectic could be expressed using the concepts and jargon of metapsychology. However, confession and forgiveness are terms that are more immediate, and close to everyday experience. That is why I have discussed them here, and of course also to continue the intertextual dialogue on the topic of arrogance.

On the metapsychological level, on the other hand, which is the one investigated by Freud and post-Freudian psychoanalysis, the ethical life thus configured corresponds to the intuition of harmony, necessary for existence between conscious and unconscious life. We can safely say that there is no field of knowledge that more than psychoanalysis has put at the center of its investigation *libido*, Eros, or the logic of *Liebe* for the fact of extending the Sophoclean vision, which would otherwise remain merely allegorical, and the Hegelian one, which otherwise would remain merely speculative, to the not only theoretical but also empirical domain of an effective practice of therapy.

Notes

1 T. Pinkard, *Hegel's Phenomenology: The Sociality of Reason* (Cambridge: Cambridge University Press, 1994), 363.

2 Cf. J. Lacan, *The Seminars of Jacques Lacan, Book XI: The Four Fundamental Concepts of Psychoanalysis* [1973], transl. A. Sheridan (New York: W. W. Norton & Company, 1978).

3 Cf. M. Heidegger, *Being and Time*, [1927], transl. J. Stambaugh (New York: State University of New York, 1996), §46, 219, 220: "something is always still *outstanding* [*aussteth*] in Dasein which has not yet become 'real' as a potentiality-of-its-being. A *constant unfinished quality* [*ständige Unabgeschlossenheit*] thus lies in the essence of the constitution of Da-sein".

4 A touching example of successful recognition can be found in L. Tolstoy's short story *The Death of Ivan Ilyich*, transl. R. Pevear (New York: Vintage Books, 2012). Sick and about to die, Ivan Ilyich discovers, in his devotion and sense of pity towards him, that only his servant, Gerasim, sees him as a person and notices his suffering, and he reciprocates with a feeling of affection and gratitude. When the protagonist realizes the indifference of his wife and daughter, he feels a sense of *astonishment* that soon turns to *dismay*. In essence, he rediscovers himself as completely helpless and dependent on others, like a small child on its mother. This topical moment of pain seems to be inherent in all the transformations we have theorized or depicted so far. It is the moment when the

master and the servant (Creon and Antigone, Bertin and Rameau, etc.) realize their own and everyone else's loneliness in the face of death. It is only from the experience of this feeling that the source of recognition can be triggered. Affection testifies to the fact that not only the intellect but also the body 'has understood'. In Heidegger, this insight becomes the meditation on the concept of authenticity. He who lives an authentic life, i.e. who is the master of himself and of his own existence, is the one who, having experienced this shock and having therefore been touched by anxiety, discovers that he lives in a certain way, but that he could also live differently; that is, he feels that he is free, that he has the possibility to choose. As he writes in *Being and Time*, 188: "Anxiety reveals in Dasein its *being toward* its own most potentiality of being, that is, *being free for* the freedom of choosing and grasping itself. Anxiety brings Dasein before its *being free for ... (propensio in)*, the authenticity of its being as possibility which it always already is. But, at the same time, it is this being to which Dasein as being-in-the-world is entrusted." With respect to the Heideggerian parameter of authentic life, J.-J- Koo ("Heidegger's Underdeveloped conception of the undistinguishedness (*Indifferenz*) of everyday human existence", in *From Conventionalism to Social Authenticity. Heidegger's Anyone and Contemporary Social Theory*, eds. H. B. Schmid and G. Thonauser (Cham, CH: Springer, 2017), 53–78, observes that for the individual there are three possible paths. There are those who live all their lives quietly in the conformity of the social group to which they belong, like sleepwalkers (*Indifferenz/undistinguishedness*); those who experience shock and manage to escape from indistinctness (*Eigentlichkeit/ownedness*); and finally, those who, having had the opportunity, opt instead for inauthenticity (*Uneigentlichkeit/unownedness*) or to escape from the feeling of distress. In the language of psychoanalysis, the anguish that gives access to *Eigentlichkeit* could be compared to the Kleinian concept of depressive position, which implies for the subject the recomposition of a split and the return to a functioning more based on the principle of reality. In Bion's terms, the dilemma facing the subject is whether to avoid or to experience emotions. On this, cf. A. Ferro, 2007, *Avoiding Emotions, Living Emotions*, transl. I. Harvey (2007, London: Routledge, 2012).

5 J. Derrida, "Avowing—The Impossible: "Returns," Repentance, and Reconciliation [——]," in, ed., *Living Together: Jacques Derrida's Communities of Violence and Peace*, ed. E. Weber, 18–41, 31: "what is occurring [*ce qui se passe*] *today* in the world, a kind of general rehearsal [*répétition*], a scene, even a theatrical rendering [*théâtralisation*] of avowal, od return, and of repentance [...] scenes of avowal are multiplied and have been accelerating for a few years, months, weeks, every day in truth, in a public space transformed by tele-technologies and by media capital, by the speed and the reach of communication, but also by the multiple effects of a technology, a techno-politics and a techno-genetics that unsettle [*bouleversent*] *at once* all conditions: conditions of being together [...] *and* the conditions of the living in its technological relation to the nonliving [...] all these scenes of avowal [...] appeal to the testimony, even to the judgment of a

community [...] instituted as an infinite court or a world confessional". Confession and forgiveness should lead to reconciliation and reparation (or healing), but instead they become a new source of cleavage and hatred, a new assertion of power; "under the pretext of transparency, a new inquisitorial obsession that transforms anybody into a subject or a defendant summoned to 'live together' according to the ensemble, while renouncing not only what one names with the old name of 'private life,' the invisible practice of faith, and so on; but also, and quite simply, while renouncing this possibility of the secret, of separation, of solitude, of silence, and of singularity, of this interruption that remains, we have seen, the inalienable condition of 'living together,' of responsibility and of decision" (ibid., 34).

6   Cf. H. G. Gadamer, *Truth and Method* [1960], transl. J. Weinsheimer and D. G. Marshall (New York: Bloomsbury, 2013), 352: "conscience represents the spiritual side of being recognized, and the mutual self-recognition in which spirit is absolute can be attained only via confession and forgiveness".

7   Cf. D. Forti, F. Natili and G. Varchetta, *Il soggetto incompiuto. Psicosocioanalisi dell'individuo, dell'organizzazione e della polis* (Milano: Guerini, 2018).

8   At first, the patient suspects that the analyst is only interested in him because he provides him with the means to live; the analyst suspects that the patient is only interested in him as a solution to his problems and not as a person. In reality, both are seeking the love and gratitude of the other. The asymmetrical relationship of dependence does not dispense with the essential symmetry that exists at the unconscious level of mutual desire.

9   D. Alighieri, *The Divine Comedy of Dante Alighieri*, transl H. W. Longfellow (London: George Routledge and Sons, 1867, Houghton, Miffllin and Company, Boston, 1867), 18, https://archive.org/details/divinecomedyofda00 dantiala/page/18/mode/2up. But in Italian "exempts" is "perdona", which means "forgives"!

10 Freud, S. *Civilization and its Discontents*, (1930), 128. In unhappy love, Freud says, it may happen that the object devours the ego, "everything that the object does and asks for is right and blameless" (Freud, S. *Group Psychology and the Analysis of the Ego*, 1921) 113. As a result, the difference between self and object is not reduced, as when sexual satisfaction is achieved, but heightened. There is also a paradoxical inversion of the moral consciousness, which no longer applies to everything that concerns the interest of the beloved object; paradoxical because to intensify, although in the eyes of a third-party observer it would have the minus sign in front of it, is still a moral consciousness but 'specialized,' that is, put at the exclusive service of the object. It is easy to see how the game is played in the investment of love between *identification* that enriches the subject with the qualities of the object, when there is reciprocity, and impoverishment or sacrifice of the ego, when there is not such reciprocity.

11 J. Derrida, "Avowing—The Impossible: 'Returns,' Repentance, and Reconciliation" [1998],. in *Living Together: Jacques Derrida's Communities of Violence and Peace*, ed. E. Weber, 18–41, 35.

12 In his theory of affectivity, S. Freud ["Group Psychology and the Analysis of the Ego", *The Standard Edition of the Complete Psychological Works of Sigmund Freud* 18 (1921): 65–144, 90–91] credits psychoanalysis with the merit of "taking love in a 'wider' sense", which, moreover, has already been captured in language, in which in this has "a entirely justifiable piece of unification", namely, the fact that all contexts, other than those of sexual love, in which we currently use the word 'love', actually "are expressions of the same instinctual impulses".

13 A. Kojève, *Introduction à la lecture de Hegel: leçons sur la Phénoménologie de l'Esprit professées de 1933 à 1939 à l'École des Hautes Études*, (1947; Paris: Gallimard, 1980), 52.

14 G. W. F. Hegel, *The Phenomenology of the Spirit*, 12–13.

15 Cf. R. B. Brandom, *The Spirit of Trust. A Reading of Hegel's Phenomenology*, cited.

16 T. Pinkard, *Hegel's Phenomenology: The Sociality of Reason*, (Cambridge: Cambridge University Press, 1994), 124: "In Hegel's term, an agent who understands himself as part of an 'ethical life, 'of *Sittlickeit*, will also come to understand himself as a 'universal self;' his *personal* point of view on himself and the world will come to be fully congruent with his *impersonal* point of view on the same things."

17 For an analysis of curiosity viewed negatively, cf. C. Pasqualin, "Per una fenomenologia dello stupore. Heidegger e l'origine emotiva del pensare", 552: "Curiosity, not to be confused with θαυμάζειν, because the lust of seeing is divorced from understanding, aspiring only to the pleasure of that rapid enjoyment of things that glides over surfaces. The man at the mercy of curiosity loses himself in the other in order to escape from himself; in the conquest of the ever new, he procures justification for the escape from his own inconsistency. In curiosity is therefore inherent a false openness, because, where the being clings to the stranger, it simultaneously closes itself off from itself from genuine questioning. The dispersion in the multiple and the ambition of omniscience shun the patient concentration on the simple that is proper to wonder, which instead nourishes an authentic interest in things." Cf. also M. Heidegger, *History of the Concept of Time: Prolegomena*, 1979, transl T. Kiesel (Bloomington, IN: Indiana University Press, 1985), 277: "This distractive non-tarrying constitutive of Dasein includes a mode of the uprooting of Dasein, a kind of being in which it is everywhere and nowhere and where it tends to be loosed from itself. In such a curiosity, Dasein organizes a *flight from itself*". Antithetical to curiosity so understood is instead wonder.

18 T. Pinkard, *Hegel's Phenomenology: The Sociality of Reason*, 122.

19 G. W. F. Hegel, *The Phenomenology of Spirit*, 108.

20 Ibid., 389. But see also this other transl. A. V. Miller in G. W. F. Hegel, *Phenomenology of Spirit* (Oxford: Oxford University Press, 1977), 409 : "The reconciling *Yea*, in which the two 'I's let go their antithetical *existence*, is the *existence* of the 'I' which has expanded into a duality, and therein remains identical with itself,

and, in its complete externalization and opposite, possesses the certainty of itself: it is God manifested in the midst of those who know themselves in the form of pure knowledge."

21 T. Pinkard, *Hegel's Phenomenology: The Sociality of Reason*, 219–220.

22 Freud, S. *Civilization and its Discontents*, (1930), 123: "Why do our relatives, the animals, not exhibit any such cultural struggle? We do not know."

23 Cf. É. Durkheim, *The Elementary Forms of Religious Life*, [1912], transl K. E. Fields (New York: The Free Press, 1995), 266: "in a sense there is divinity in us. For society, that unique source of all that is sacred, is not satisfied to move us from outside and to affect us transitorily; it organizes itself lastingly within us. It arouses in us a whole world of ideas and feelings that express it but at the same time are an integral and permanent part of ourselves." And further (267): "The individual soul is thus only a portion of the group's collective soul. It is the anonymous force on which the cult is based but incarnated in an individual whose personality it cleaves to: It is mana individualized."

Conclusions

The starting point for this book was a theoretical and clinical interest in a category of psychotic patients who present a particular symptomatic configuration, which Bion, one of the most brilliant psychoanalytic writers, identifies as the triad of arrogance, curiosity and stupidity. For analysis, the problem of treating these patients is a challenge because they confront it, as Foucault would say, with its own will to know. The patient suffers from a split personality. The internal rupture results from the constitution of a ruthless moral consciousness that drives him to adopt an ideal of the self that is persecutory in that it is unattainable. It is the price the subject pays to reconcile with a cruel inner god. The source of the whole process is the fear of losing the object, which Freud identifies with 'evil'; the solution is the adoption of a disjunction between the material and the affective relationship.

Psychoanalysis as an institution, and consequently those who embody its principles in daily clinical work (this is Bion's position), may in certain cases function on the basis of a similar split between intellectual (hermeneutic) and emotional ('pathetic') understanding, and thus suffer from the same symptomatic triad. When it does so, it is to obey a similar, rigid need to know from a 'scientific' perspective. Although historically understandable (Freud lived in the age of positivism), such a perspective is actually a perversion of the method, since it may lead to objectifying the other; as Bion writes, to seeking the truth (what one imagines to be the truth) *at any costs* and, even with the best of intentions, to *looking down on* the patient and one's colleagues. In this way, psychoanalysis is blind on the theoretical level, even if it can achieve its goals indirectly. In fact, it does not realize that the real agent of treatment is the affective relationship (necessarily equal or symmetrical), which is established also thanks to the necessary asymmetry of roles and which allows the analytic couple to escape from unequal or dominant forms of relationship. It also tends to be dogmatic.

DOI: 10.4324/9781032669427-6

It fails to see that certain apparently inexplicable regressions in psychotic patients are caused by the treatment itself.

In carrying out these reflections, Bion moves simultaneously on several levels: he gives an example of how to overcome a clinical problem; he innovates theory; he reaffirms the value of psychoanalysis as a discipline capable of self-curation and of confronting its own dross of ideology (of 'moralism'). The vertex he uses to tie these various threads together is the myth of Oedipus. Bion reinterprets it in a way that is not only original but also unprecedented. Oedipus's guilt is not so much a sexual crime or patricide, but the impulse to know the truth at all costs. His *hýbris* (term that coincides with 'arrogance') is to delude himself that he can eliminate the Sphinx, which is the question (the enigma).

In essence, on the basis of a radical principle of intersubjectivity and a new theory of the mind and the unconscious, Bion revolutionizes psychoanalysis. In accordance with the dictates of contemporary epistemology, he radicalizes its main evolutionary line, which over the years has led it to increasingly integrate the unconscious subjectivity of the analyst into the treatment process.

In Bion's short essay from which I have taken my cue, arrogance-*hýbris* thus resonates with a much broader research agenda. Bion uses it as a powerful lens with which to clarify the structure of seemingly very distant phenomena. In this book, my intention was to rethink and enrich the results of Bion's reflections on this issue. I have tried to identify the common thread that links arrogance as a banal and widespread expression of the 'evil' and malaise of society; as a 'pathological' aspect of character; as a symptom of psychosis; to use Habermas' formula[1], as the "scientific self-misunderstanding" of psychoanalysis; finally, in its zero degree, as a constitutive factor of existence (*ek-istere* is itself an expression of *hýbris*).

Unlike literature and philosophy, psychoanalysis has also developed a practice of care. It seems to me that the principles of this practice of care and, as we have seen, of self-care, can usefully be proposed, at least in an analogous way, to contribute to a diagnosis of contemporaneity or of the so-called 'bad present'. On the one hand, already with Freud, psychoanalysis affirms itself as an authoritative critical theory—in fact, it can be said to have contributed to its foundation; on the other hand, from the beginning and with extraordinary results, precisely with Bion's analysis of the emotional functioning of groups, it postulates a substantial equivalence between the psychology of the subject and the psychology of the social community or the social subject.

The book thus began with an attempt to define and understand arrogance as a psychological trait. To do this, I used material from popular culture (the TV series ER) and literature (Shakespeare's *Henry V*, a passage from Proust's *Recherche*, the figure of Agamemnon in the *Iliad*, Tolstoy's short story *The Death of Ivan Ilyich*; and in some cases—with Sophocles' *Antigone* and Diderot's *Rameau's Nephew*—from literature already invested by the powerful beam of light from Hegel's observations in the *Phenomenology*. Hegel and some of his commentators, including especially Mancini, Pinkard, Butler, and Brandom, played a key role in guiding my reading of arrogance, which has gradually moved along a number of axes, descriptive, metapsychological, individual, social, literary and philosophical. In the third chapter I have tried to weave together some of these various threads. My thesis can be summarized as follows: it is not only the arrogant individual who suffers from an almost unintentional sociopathy, understood as an unconscious symptom-solution for the anxiety that lies at the root of the splitting of the personality that has perverted its inner world. The same split or abstract logic also explains the perversion of institutions or of society as a whole.

As a clinician, convinced that therapy is more about asking questions than giving answers, I avoid giving solutions to this problem. As Derrida says, there are no solutions; that is, there are only partial and temporary solutions. There is, however, critical thinking, which has an essential function. The innovations of technology and the consequent triumph of the ideology of technology, that is to say, the affirmation of a rationality that tends to absolutize the efficiency of procedures and the achievement of abstract results in the various forms of life of sociality, always create new forms of relations of domination. The task of critical theory, and if possible of an integrated critical theory, is to identify them in order to constitute *points of resistance* in defense of human dignity. If I am not proposing solutions, I am proposing, by way of parable or allegory, some reflections on Winnicott's concept of "safe space", also in relation to current issues such as the Covid-19 pandemic. Anyone could read in them suggestions for other practices of "care" that are not those of analysis.

The essence of what I have tried to express in this book, also by virtue of its deliberately intertextual character, is the need, each time, to return from thinking in binary oppositions to dialectical thinking. In essence, it is about overcoming the caesura between good and bad critical theory, past and present, power and counter-power, community and individual, psychology of the subject and psychology of society. As we know from clinical work, caesuras can be crossed when the logic of love takes precedence over the logic of abstraction. It is based on equal, balanced, symmetrical relationships, which must therefore be allowed to develop, although they must also remain to some extent asymmetrical.

At the social level, it is difficult to say what kind of practice this discourse can be translated into. However, in very general terms, anything that helps to rediscover the sense of "we" or "we-ness", as in analysis, even before anything is said or done, changes the emotional climate and makes it more hospitable. When this happens, anxiety decreases and with it the need to resort to the logic of abstraction. All those occasions in community life which create the conditions for getting to know each other, for becoming familiar with each other, and thus for becoming less afraid of what at first sight seems alien to us, go in this direction. Just one example, but an important one. The opportunity for university students to spend a year abroad is an initiative that is widely recognized as valuable. It is a beautiful, concrete and simple example of the operationalization of the non-secessionist logic of love.

The Europe in which Freud wrote *Civilisation and Its Discontents* was emerging from the catastrophe of the First World War and was heading for an even worse one. In the same Europe, with the tragic exception of the war in the Balkans in the 1990s, we are coming out of seventy years of prosperity and peace, something that has never happened in the course of history. However, we are witnessing a resurgence of destructive pressures (nationalism, populism, short-sighted selfishness), as if the memory of the great tragedies of the last century had been erased. For this reason, it is worth reflecting more, if possible, but not in the sterile form of moral condemnation, which has always been one of the most successful disguises, on the mask of banality, for example as arrogance, with which violence (evil), before spreading like wildfire, begins to infiltrate our everyday lives inadvertently.

Notes

1 J. Habermas, *Knowledge and Human Interest*, [1968], transl. by J. J. Shapiro, Cambridge, Uk, Polity Press, 1987, 214. On this issue, Ricoeur, (*On Psychoanalysis*, [2008], Cambridge, UK, Polity Press) argues that the question of the hermeneutic status of psychoanalysis arose from the failure of all attempts to treat psychoanalysis as an observational science among others, essentially as a natural science.

2 *The Death of Ivan Ilyich*, New York, Vintage Books, 2012)., transl. by R. Pevear.

Made in the USA
Middletown, DE
08 March 2024